# FRUITS & NUTS
## in Symbolism & Celebration

**Mary Reed**

Resource Publications, Inc.
San Jose, California

Editorial director: Kenneth Guentert
Managing editor: Elizabeth J. Asborno
Illustrator: Kathi Drolet
Cover design and production: Huey Lee
Front cover photo: Perry Chow
Back cover photo: Eric Mayer

© 1992 Mary Reed. All rights reserved. No part of this book may be photocopied or otherwise reproduced without written permission. For reprint permission, write to:

Reprint Department
Resource Publications, Inc.
160 E. Virginia Street #290
San Jose, California 95112-5876

**Library of Congress Cataloging in Publication Data**
Reed, Mary, 1945-
    Fruits and nuts in symbolism and celebration / Mary Reed.
       p.    cm.
    Includes bibliographical references and index.
    ISBN 0-89390-252-7 — ISBN 0-89390-238-1 (pbk.)
    1. Fruit—Folklore. 2. Nuts—Folklore. 3. Food—Symbolic aspects. I. Title.
GR790.F78R44 1992
398'.355—dc20                                    92-23681

96 95 94 93 92 | 5 4 3 2 1

# Contents

# Acknowledgments

Many people helped in the compilation of information for this book, and, to all of them, my thanks. I must particularly acknowledge the assistance of the staff of the reference department of the Lincoln Library, Springfield, Illinois, for their cheerful labors in finding answers to the nigh impossible questions I posed them.

To Borg and Ishmael, for monolithic assistance; and to the Crabapple Crew, who gave generously of their time and knowledge, and who, upon hearing about the project, heroically forbore from sending me baskets of pomegranates (folly)—if a book such as this may have a dedication, then let it be to them; to my parents, Mick and Mary Reed; to all the Reedies; and to Julia Stone, from "the scribbler in the garret."

# Introduction

It was surely serendipity that I was offered almond and cherry tea at a celebration announcing a new baby some years ago, for it was not until researching this book that I realized how appropriate was the choice. Among other things, almonds represent fatherhood, and cherries have connections with birth in more than one culture.

Fruits and nuts have religious, ethnic, social, and symbolic significance, which renders them a rich source of inspiration for ritual and celebration. What, for example, could be more appropriate for a baby shower than a dish of apples and pomegranates, representing, as they do, knowledge of fertility? A post-funeral meal might offer blackberries (sorrow) but could equally include quinces (resurrection). Oranges (glory) and pears (divine love) are appropriate for Easter Sunday, while hazels and tangerines (rain and sun symbols, respectively) have their place in harvest festival gatherings.

Some of the celebration and symbolism suggestions in this book come from the Victorian flower language, which conveyed sentiments and messages by the use of certain flowers. The modern floral language does the same; however, the Victorian one was more extensive, both in its messages and the flowers used, many of which belonged to the fruit family. The more limited Japanese floral calendar is also referenced here, using blossoms traditionally connected with the months as their symbol (usually, but not always, the time when the flowers are in bloom), as will be noted in such entries as, for example, **cherry**.

Although most fruits and nuts are available year-round, whether fresh, frozen, dried, preserved, or canned, or as juice, wine, or flavored teas, their use is not limited to the culinary. You can, for example, also do the following:

- Decorate with them. An arrangement of several symbolic fruits and/or nuts as a centerpiece can be echoed by smaller versions at place-settings.

- Use their greenery and/or blossoms for floral decorations such as bouquets, wreaths (not just for funerals), swags, buttonholes, and so on.

- Mark an occasion by planting an appropriate tree. I have done so on several family occasions, the last being a crabapple for our departed parents.

- Use hollowed-out fruits as containers, perhaps in suitable shapes: a melon can be made into a football helmet, a pumpkin into a baby buggy, a watermelon into a ship. Smaller fruits—apples, oranges—work well for candleholders or vases. Larger specimens—pineapples, melons—are suitable for holding floral centerpieces or symbolic fruit salads.

- Present as a gift, perhaps by creating your own symbolic basket of fruits and nuts.

- Draw upon the meanings noted in this book for conversation among friends.

- Light appropriately scented candles, widely available in gift and stationery shops, and often sold molded in the shape of the chosen fruit.

- Create items with the appropriate fruit or nut connected to the celebration—an invitation to a summer solstice party written on stationery with a strawberry motif (emblematic of June's full moon), or perhaps a toy crafted of walnut (a symbol of childhood) for the child who has just begun kindergarten. During the writing of this book, I came across (without any particular search) a wide range of such creations, including those shaped like, or with a motif of, apples (ceramic box, glass ornament); grapes (earrings, bracelet); lemons (ornament, bath salts); peaches (notecards, soap); pineapples (perfume jar, ice bucket—the latter being particularly appropriate, given the fruit's traditional meaning of hospitality); pumpkins (lamp, teapot); and watermelons (glassware, bowl, candleholder).

The index of occasions keyed to fruits and nuts is, of course, by no means exhaustive, but nonetheless it is my hope that it will provide an inspirational cornucopia, acting as a springboard for those seeking new and special ways to enhance observances of the seasons, stages and celebrations occurring along the road of life.

Since some of the fruits and nuts are sacred to more than one religion, their placement in the text is based solely upon which seemed most appropriate. Bold-faced names of fruits/nuts refer the reader to other useful entries.

# FRUITS

# *Apple*

One of the most common fruits in folklore and legend—often with connections to the afterlife—apples are thought to have originated in the Black Sea area. The fruit gave its name to the genus *Malus,* "apple tree." Its common name derives from the Old English *aeppel* via the Indo-European name for the fruit, *abol.*

Christian   Although the fruit is not actually named, apples are popularly regarded as having been the fruit of the Tree of Knowledge (see also **banana, fig, lemon, orange, pomegranate, quince, tomato**). In Christian art, the apple represents Eve, sin, temptation, and the Fall (appropriately, the Latin *malum* means both "apple" and "evil").* It is for this reason that the larynx is popularly known as the Adam's apple, a piece supposedly having stuck in his throat, while an "apple eater" is one who is easily led astray.** If shown with a **gourd** (see **melon**), emblematic of protection or rejection of evil, the apples are being rejected as symbols of evil or temptation.

Beautifully scented apple blossoms symbolize Mary, and a French legend has it that an apple tree offered its fruit to her unborn child, a story recalling the well-known *Cherry Tree Carol* (see also **cherry**).

Apples and cucumbers, a member of the **gourd** (see **melon**) family, appear in Carlo Crivelli's *Madonna and Child* (c. 1480). In this painting, the cucumbers are taken to refer to Jonah's **gourd** (Jonah 4) and to symbolize resurrection, while the apple is emblematic of sin, from whose taint Mary is free (for other Marian symbolism, see also **almond, cherry, lemon, olive, raspberry, strawberry, walnut**).

On a tree of Paradise (see also **cherry, peach, plum**), apples symbolize redemption. It may well be for this reason that they are mentioned in a traditional children's song sung door-to-door on All Souls Day (see also **cherry, pear, plum**).

---

\*   Robert Quillen, editor, writer, and wit, erected an obelisk under an apple tree in Fountain Inn, South Carolina, as a memorial to Eve, on the grounds that he was related to her on his mother's side.

\*\*  "Adam's apple" was also applied to the **grapefruit**.

A basket of apples and roses symbolizes St. Dorothy, from the story that they appeared in response to a mocking request for fruit and flowers from heaven, which was shouted at her as she went to her execution. Three golden apples (sometimes interpreted as **oranges**) represent St. Nicholas. In his commentary on Song of Songs 2:5, St. Bernard writes that the apple's blossoms refer to faith and its fruit to good works.[*]

**Ethnic**   Up to the last century, some Bavarian villages enacted a mock battle between Winter and Summer on the fourth Sunday in Lent. Winter appeared in heavy clothing, while Summer carried a flowering branch or small tree decorated with apples and **pears**. After a procession, Winter was symbolically vanquished. In parts of the Tyrol, palm staffs of willow decorated with apples, pretzels, and ribbons were carried in procession on Palm Sunday. In other areas, crowns of silver fir decorated with eggs, apples, and religious pictures were displayed on the same day.

It was once the custom to wassail orchards in western English counties (especially Devon and Somerset, famous for cider) during the Christmas holidays or on Twelfth Night. Apple trees were serenaded and splashed with cider, and sometimes pieces of bread were left for the "robin" or tree spirit. The idea was to encourage trees to bear good crops. The traditional Christmas wassail punch (from Old English *was hael*, "be hale" or "be in good health") was cider, usually with roasted apples floating in it. A similar custom intended to induce fruit trees to bear well was practiced in parts of southern Belgium on the first two Sundays of Lent, when flaming torches were waved around the branches of apple, **cherry**, and **pear** trees.

---

[*]  It has also been suggested that **apricots**, symbols of the yoni (female genitalia), are meant in this passage.

Apples are popular Christmas decorations in Norway. They are one of three traditional toe-stuffers for Christmas stockings (the other two being nuts and an **orange** or **tangerine**). An apple sometimes replaced the **orange** (which some saw as a symbol for the sun at the mid-winter solstice) in the mouth of the Yuletide roast boar.

It was a pleasant custom in one Swiss canton to plant an apple tree to mark the birth of a boy (see also **coconut, pear**).

The widespread cultivation of the apple provided many nicknames for other fruits. The **citron** was known as the "Median apple"; **peaches** were called "Persian apples"; the Cornish refer to **peaches** today as "suede apples"; the word **"melon"** is derived from the Greek *melopepon*, "apple **gourd**." The Romans called **pomegranates** "Carthaginian apples," after the fruit's supposed city of origin. **Tomatoes**—an alleged aphrodisiac—were "love apples"* and were also once known in Germany as the *Paradies apfel*, "Paradise apple." To the French, potatoes are "earth apples" (*pommes de terre*), a phrase also applied by ancient Egyptians to chamomile, regarded as sacred.

In British folklore, those apple-johns (or john-apples; see Literary/Artistic) picked around St. John's Day are said to have extraordinary keeping powers, remaining edible for two years and tasting best when shriveled up. Some, however, advised that apples not be picked before St. Swithin's Day in July, for rain falling then doubly blessed the fruit (as well as predicted forty more days of wet weather).

Apples are a Romany (Gypsy) love-gift and are offered at their weddings, while it is said that Byzantine emperors chose their brides by presenting them with an apple.

---

* "Love-apple" was also applied to the mandrake and eggplant.

The Hittite Law Code stated that should an apple tree be destroyed by fire, a new one had to be planted and the culprit fined five shekels (reduced to three, if he/she were a slave). Similar provisions protected the **grape**vine and **pomegranate**, a measure of their importance to the society.

## Judaic

Apple slices dipped in honey are eaten during Rosh Hashanah (Hebrew for "head of the year," i.e., the New Year) in hopes for a sweet twelve-month to follow.

One of the traditional foods for Pesach ("to pass over," i.e., Passover) is haroset (loosely, "clay"), a mixture of apple, nuts, wine, and spices, representing the bricks and mortar with which the Children of Israel were forced to build for their captors during their captivity in Egypt (see also **date, raisin** [in **grape**]).

Joel 1:7, 12 characterizes desolated Israel as having fruitless apple, **fig**, and **pomegranate** trees, **date** palms, and **grape**vines.

Proverbs 25:11 describes a fit word as a golden apple.

## Literary/Artistic

In the medieval ballad about Thomas the Rhymer, the Lady of Elphame (the underworld) warns him against eating apples there because the fruit contained "hell's plagues." The implication is that, if he ate of these apples, he would have to remain there. A similar role is played by the **pomegranate** in the stories of Persephone and Proserpine (see also **peach**).

It has been said that apples played a prominent role in the paintings of French artist Paul Cezanne (see also **watermelon**).

The apple's connection with good health is well known and recalled in such folk sayings as, "An apple before bed / Makes doctors beg for bread," while the old rhyme, "Whoever plants an apple may well see it end / Whoever plants a **pear** plants it for his friends" (or variants) compares the longevity of the two types of fruit trees.

Shakespeare used apples as a synonym for aged looks in *Henry IV, Part I* (1598), in which a character's face is compared to "an old apple-john" (see Ethnic).

Colloquially, "Apples of Sodom" or "Dead Sea fruit" refer to something which, when achieved, turns out to be a hollow sham or disappointment. It has been suggested that the term was inspired by an old folktale that the water of the Dead Sea was so bitter it killed all the vegetation around it, or by the vine of Sodom, which bore bitter **grapes** (Deuteronomy 32:32).

"A rotten apple spoils the barrel" is self-explanatory, while the "apple of one's eye," meaning something especially dear to one, was derived from references to the iris in, for example, Psalms 17:8 and Proverbs 7:2.

In underworld argot common in the 1950s, an "apple" was the victim of a crime, perhaps a reference to the expulsion from Eden.

From the sixteenth century onward, "won with an apple, lost with a nut," or vice-versa, has referred to someone who is indecisive or easily swayed.

The British "apple-pie bed" (known to Americans as a "short-sheeted" one) was derived from the French *nappe pliee,* "folded sheets."

"Apple-pie order" means everything neatly arranged, while "Mom's apple pie" is synonymous with American family life. (If there was a national fruit for America, it would be either the apple, **cherry**, or **cranberry**.)

"Comparing apples to **oranges**" is singularly fruitless because, by virtue of their different natures, there is no common ground for comparison.

"Upsetting the applecart" means to cause chaos or disrupt the natural order of things (see also **gooseberry**).

In heraldry, green roundels resembling small apples are called "pomeys" or "pomeis."

## Mythologicial

Because apples were sacred to love goddesses such as Greek Aphrodite, Roman Venus, and Babylonian Ishtar, they figure in a number of marriage divination charms. One is to throw a piece of apple peel over the left shoulder; when it falls on the floor, the peel will supposedly form the initial of the future spouse. Another charm is to squeeze apple seeds between the fingers; the direction in which they fly indicates that from which the seeker's lover will appear. A third involves combing the hair while looking in a mirror and eating an apple; the face of the future mate will then appear reflected next to the watcher's.

Apples are said to keep better if picked under a waning moon, a belief which may be connected to the fact that they are sacred to the virginal moon goddess Diana, whose festival was celebrated by the Romans on August 13 with feasts at which cakes, roast kid, and apples were eaten (see also **orange, pear**).

In Norse mythology, the goddess Iduna was in charge of the Apples of Immortality, food of the gods. It is implied in an eleventh-century poem that the Scandinavian departed eat Apples of Hel in the underworld, Hel being the goddess who rules there. Two types of apples (as well as **hazels, walnuts**, and other food) were found among grave goods on a pagan ship-burial in Oseberg, Norway.

In Celtic legend, King Cormac is given three wishes represented by three golden apples on one bough, but loses his family temporarily because of them. It was to the misty Isle of Avalon (usually translated as "Isle of Apples" or "Apple Orchards") that the Celtic hero and high king Arthur sailed to be cured of his mortal wounds.

Greek mythology tells of the beautiful princess Atalanta, who would not marry until a suitor won a foot-race against her. Hippomenes won by dropping, one at a time, three golden apples (a gift from Aphrodite, goddess of love), delaying Atalanta, who could not resist picking them up.

It was for the Apple of Discord, engraved "For the Fairest," that Hera, queen of the gods, Athene, goddess of wisdom, and Aphrodite competed. Paris awarded it to Aphrodite, who had promised him Helen, an action which ultimately led to the Trojan War. (The Victorian flower language recalls this in allotting apple blossoms the symbolism of preference or choice.)

The golden apples of the Garden of the Hesperides were a wedding gift to Hera when she married Zeus, and it was one of the Twelve Labors of Hercules to steal some. He accomplished this by trickery, but the apples were later restored to their rightful owner by Athene. This Garden lay to the west (Hesperus was the evening star, but it was his daughters, aided by a dragon, who guarded the Garden) and was also known as the Isle of the Blest, another name for Paradise.

Nemesis, Greek goddess of divine and inescapable retribution, was sometimes shown carrying apple branches as a reminder of death, which comes to all.

Greek gardeners offered apples, **figs, grapes, quinces**, and vegetables to Priapus, god of male regenerative powers, to obtain his protection for their crops.

Apples, **figs**, and **grapes** were held sacred to Greek Dionysus as patron of trees as well as of wine and merriment.

"Star apple" refers to the shape revealed when an apple is cut in half horizontally; this made the fruit sacred to the Earth or Mother Goddess.

## Symbolic Uses of the Apple

- Recalling Christian symbolism of redemption, appropriate for All Saints Day; baptism; confirmation; Easter Sunday; first eucharist; pilgrimage

- Recalling Marian symbolism, appropriate for Christmas; Epiphany; Marian festivals

- Recalling Victorian symbolism of preference/choice, appropriate for new citizen

- Recalling symbolism in Christian art, appropriate for feast days of Sts. Dorothy and Nicholas

- Recalling begging song, appropriate for All Souls Day

- Recalling Swiss custom, plant an apple tree to mark the adoption, birth, or birthday of a boy

- Recalling Romany love-gift and the apple's sacredness to love goddesses, appropriate for bridal shower; engagement; Friendship Day; remarriage; St. Valentine's Day; wedding; wedding anniversary

- Recalling connection with Eve, Mother of All Living, appropriate for adoption; baby shower; grandmother's birthday; Grandparent's Day; mother's birthday; Mother's Day; mother-in-law's birthday; Mother-in-Law's Day; also appropriate for feast day of St. Monica, patron of mothers

- Recalling connection with Tree of Knowledge, appropriate for beginning kindergarten/college/ school; commencement; graduation; reaching adulthood

- Recalling Judaic symbolism of New Year hopes, appropriate for New Year's Day; New Year's Eve

- Recalling Bavarian victory of summer, appropriate for Midsummer's Day; Midsummer's Eve; summer solstice

- Recalling apple's sacredness to the Earth/Mother Goddess, appropriate for women's festivals

- Recalling "apple-pie order," appropriate for an audit

- Recalling connection with moon-goddess, appropriate for full moon; lunar eclipse; new/quarter moon

- Recalling connection with good health, appropriate for get well soon; recovery; also appropriate for feast days of Sts. Luke, patron of physicians, Camillus, patron of nurses, and saints invoked against illnesses

- Recalling connection with the fate of humankind to work after the Fall, appropriate for Bosses Day; feast days of Sts. Joseph, patron of workers, and Zita, patron of servants; Labor Day; May Day (a traditional holiday for workers); Secretaries' Day

- Recalling connection with the afterlife, appropriate for anniversary of loss; birthday of departed; celebration of life; funeral; Memorial Day; remembering departed; wake

- Recalling Tyrolean custom, appropriate for Palm Sunday

# Apricot

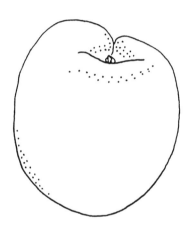

Although the apricot seems to have originated in China, it was once thought to be a native of Armenia, a belief reflected in its botanical name, *Prunus armeniaca,* "**plum** of Armenia." The apricot's common name has been derived variously from the Latin *apricus,* "sun-loving," *apricatio,* "sun-basking," and *praecoquus,* meaning, loosely, "early-ripening" (hence, "precocious").

**Ethnic**

The apricot is a staple among the Hunzukut of the mountainous region along the Chinese/Pakistani border. It is said that Hunzukut women refuse to live where no apricots grow.

In Chinese symbolism, the apricot represents timidity.

By virtue of its shape, the main symbolism of the apricot is of the yoni (female genitalia; see also **almond, fig, grape, pomegranate**). It has therefore been suggested that the **apple** in Song of Songs 2:5 refers to the apricot. Appropriately, Europeans once regarded the fruit as an aphrodisiac, and to dream of it is an excellent omen, promising the sleeper good fortune, especially in love.

The sixteenth-century English herbalist William Turner stated in his 1551 herbal that "Abracockes...are less than the other peches," and although the tree can live up to a century, it is not robust.

**Literary/Artistic**

During a scene set in the Duke of York's garden in Shakespeare's *Richard II* (1595), a gardener give instructions that hanging "apricocks" be bound up, likening their heaviness on the branches to someone's offspring weighing them down.

A traditional nursery rhyme equates July with rain, apricots, and gilly-flowers.

**Mythological**

A Babylonian medical text includes the story that, when Creation was complete, the worm supplicated the sun god Shamash for food. Shamash offered it apricots and **figs**, but the worm rejected both and instead took up residence in humankind's teeth and gums, thus becoming the ancestor of toothaches. The text recommends treating the ailment by telling the story three times and then offering prayers (see also **olive, walnut**).

## Symbolic Uses of the Apricot

- Recalling Babylonian legend, appropriate for first tooth and for feast day of St. Apollonia, invoked against toothaches

- Recalling alleged aphrodisiac properties, appropriate for St. Valentine's Day

- Recalling symbolism of the yoni and thus femininity, appropriate for girl's birthday; women's festivals

- Recalling connection with July and rain, and the tradition that rain on his feast day foretells forty more wet days, appropriate for St. Swithin's Day

- Recalling Latin derivations, appropriate for planting; summer solstice

- Recalling dream omen of good fortune, appropriate for good fortune; housewarming; new home; new job; new venture; New Year's Day; New Year's Eve; remarriage; wedding

# Banana

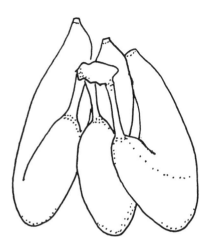

Though popularly considered a fruit, the banana is, in fact, an herb and can thus symbolize misunderstanding and, by extension, the overcoming of it. The banana is thought to have originated in southeast Asia, possibly on the Indian sub-continent. Its common name is derived from the Congolese name, *banana*, grown on the banano tree. Its botanical name, *Musa sapienta*, may be translated "Muse of the wise men" ("muse" meaning the intellectual or artistic spirit, and "wise men" referring to the Indian yogis debating in its shade, according to an old folk-tale). However, for reasons now apparently lost, it is more commonly connected with Antonius Musa, physician of the Roman emperor Augustus. In either case wisdom is strongly suggested, which contrasts with the banana's modern connotations.

**Christian**   Bananas have male symbolism for obvious reasons and have thus been suggested as the fruit of the Tree of Knowledge (see also **apple, fig, lemon, orange, pomegranate, quince, tomato**). The banana was once known as "Adam's **fig**," and a species growing in the Indies is colloquially known as the "**fig** banana" (see also **date**).

**Ethnic**   In Melanesia, bananas are taboo for bereaved relatives during the mourning period. Malayan post-natal ritual included offering new mothers a salad of banana, fish, **coconut**, and various fruits for three days after the birth (see also **date, orange**). Some Pacific fishermen say bringing home bananas aboard ship brings bad luck. In parts of Asia, the banana flower is considered a delicacy, dried bananas are a popular candy on the Cook Islands, and fried bananas are relished in Singapore.

In Thailand, small banana-leaf boats carrying a lit candle and flowers are launched on rivers during the November festival of Loy Krathong (Thai, loosely, "letting go of the small vessels"). It is believed that these little boats take away one's troubles as they float downriver.

The Lua people of Thailand offer flowers enclosed in packets of banana leaves to the spirits.

In Samoa, banana leaf plates were taboo to those families to whom the tree was sacred, for fear that touching them would cause divine wrath. Similarly, Solomon Islanders would not eat the fruit of certain banana trees thought to be the dwelling places of departed souls. In some Pacific islands, bananas were regarded as the fruit of the Tree of Life.

In parts of Papua New Guinea, bananas are among foods exchanged in rituals held in honor of elders who have died.

The folk theater performances of the Gimi people of New Guinea's highland country include men dressed in bamboo masks and banana leaf hats, portraying cockatoos (which represent dead relatives of actors playing hunters). Banana leaf hats are also worn during initiation rites of the Small Nambas tribe of the New Hebrides.

The Mru (or Murung) people of Bangladesh hold an annual two-day festival at which a cow is sacrificed and eaten. This commemorates when the god Torai gave religious and moral instructions to all of humankind except the Mru. The tribe therefore sent a cow to Torai, asking for similar guidelines, which the god wrote on banana leaves to send back to them. However, on its journey home, the cow ate the leaves; thus, ever since, the tribe takes its annual revenge upon the cow's descendants.

The banana was once considered a very exotic fruit, as it was not generally known to the American public until it was sold for 10 cents apiece at the 1876 Pennsylvania Centennial Exhibition. Thus, until that time, it symbolized faraway places (see also **coconut**).

## Literary/Artistic

Josephine Baker scandalized Paris between the wars with her exotic *Danse Bananes* (French, "Banana Dance"), in which her costume consisted largely—and not very largely at that—of a skirt made of bananas.

Frank Silver and Irving Cohn, whose "Yes, We Have No Bananas" (1923) was wildly popular on both sides of the Atlantic in the period between the wars and is still sung today, would probably have been surprised to hear an anti-tariff song parodying their lyrics. The new version appeared during a campaign for a British general election the same year, when taxes on certain imported items were a particularly bitter issue. (The parody claimed that food would cost more if the taxes were passed.)

Australians use the term "banana oil" in the same sense as Americans say "snake oil salesman." The British colloquialism "to feel a right 'nana" means to feel foolish (see also **lemon**). The phrase may be connected with the banana skin of slapstick comedy or possibly music-hall slang (see next paragraph).

The term "top banana" of an organization (rapidly being displaced in popular slang by "top gun") is supposedly derived from a music-hall routine in which a trio of comedians take turns delivering the punchline while waving a banana. From this came "second banana," a deputy or underling.* "Going bananas" is the herbal equivalent of "going nuts," perhaps connected with the man-handling meted out to the "third banana" in music-hall routines.

Perhaps the banana's strangest claim to fame is that upon eating one, the schoolboy Eric becomes Bananaman in the children's comic strip of the same name.

---

\* In October 1990, an Associated Press report about the introduction of a new sidekick in the *Batman* comic strip was headlined: "Holy Second Banana! New Robin Hatched!"

## Symbolic Uses of the Banana

- Recalling connotation of faraway places, appropriate for bon voyage; launching

- Recalling symbolism of male vigor and thus masculinity, appropriate for boy's birthday; men's festivals; remarriage; wedding

- Recalling music-hall routine's "top banana," appropriate for promotion; reaching a goal

- Recalling symbolism of overcoming misunderstanding, appropriate for negotiation; peace celebration; reconciliation

# *Blackberry*

Also known as the bramble, the blackberry's common name is self-descriptive. Its botanical name, *Rubus fruiticosus*, means "blackberry bush" or "bramble shrub." Blackberries are native to Europe.

**Christian**   Luke 6:44 mentions the bramble in a parable meaning people are known by their works (see also **fig, grape**). Matthew uses a similar analogy (7:15-16) in warning against false prophets.

In Christian art the blackberry is sometimes used to represent spiritual neglect or ignorance.

Mid-Mediterranean folklore states that blackberry runners were used to make the Crown of Thorns and that the darkness of the berries symbolizes drops of Christ's blood. Another legend explains that the blackberry was beautiful until cursed by Lucifer, who fell into a bramble upon his expulsion from heaven. According to Devonshire folklore, he re-enters the berries each September 30, which is the time they ripen and darken. More about this below.

**Ethnic**   Blackberries, like **elderberries**, have a bad reputation in folklore and are regarded in general as a fruit of ill omen. In Europe, blackberries are considered death fruits and have strong connections with wicca.* In Brittany, it was considered best to leave the fruit alone, as they were viewed as "untouchable" fairy fruit (see also **elderberry, pear**).

In England, Blackberry Summer was that time around the end of September and beginning of October when the fruit ripened (see Christian). However, in the Creek Indian calendar, it was June that was known as the Blackberry Month (see also **chestnut, strawberry**; see Literary/Artistic).

Blackberries symbolize sorrow in general as well as the painful side of affairs of the heart.

---

\* Wicca is a pre-Christian religion, which is now generally, though erroneously, known as witchcraft.

| Judaic | Judges 9:8-15 relates a parable concerning a non-royal claimant to the throne. **Fig, grape**vine, and **olive** are offered the Kingship of the Trees, but all refuse for various reasons. The humble bramble, however, agrees to accept the honor. |
|---|---|

Among numerous folk remedies mentioned in the Talmud (Hebrew, meaning "study," "learning"), it is noted that intestinal worms can be treated with scrapings of bramble and cynodon roots or bramble parings boiled in beer (see also **date**).

| Literary/Artistic | Blackberries were reportedly a taboo food for the Celts, although they enjoyed blackberry wine. For this reason, in his reconstructed Druid Tree Alphabet,\* Robert Graves gives the blackberry as an alternative to the non-native **grape**vine as the "tree" of the tenth month, beginning September 2, and representing the letter "M" (see also **elderberry, hazel**.) |
|---|---|

In *Song of Myself* (1855), Walt Whitman mused on the possibility of blackberries decorating heavenly parlors.

Proverbially, the berry means haste, after the story of the man so eager to pick berries that he leapt into a blackberry bush, losing his eyesight to the thorns, although happily receiving it back upon leaping out.

A character in Shakespeare's *Henry IV, Part I* (1598) states that even if reasons were as numerous as blackberries, still he would not give one if an attempt was made to make him do so. Here the fruit has become connected with the courage of one's convictions, or obstinancy, depending upon the viewpoint.

---

\* For this brilliant but controversial reconstruction, see Graves' *White Goddess*.

The "prickelie bushe" of the traditional song is commonly identified with the blackberry, though some have suggested the hawthorn tree. In this song, a condemned man (or, in some versions, a maiden) asks each member of his family in turn to save him by bribing the hangman. All decline, stating with somewhat unseemly relish that they have gathered with the express intention of seeing him executed. At the last moment, however, he is saved by his lover, with whom he leaves (in some versions, after cursing his family), vowing never again to get into the prickelie bushe, that is, the trouble which brought him to the gallows in the first place. Thus, the blackberry symbolizes remorse (see also **elderberry, raspberry**).

Like the **fig** and **tomato**, blackberries also represent lust, and indeed lust and blackberries are mentioned within three words of each other in "Phillada Flouts Me," an anonymous seventeenth-century poem printed in *Wit Restored* (1658).

## Medicinal

An old English cure for ruptures, according to Gloucestershire natives, was to walk under an arch of blackberry runners. In Cornwall, blackberry poultices were used to treat swellings.

The fruit was recommended for invalids with delicate digestions, while the seventeenth-century herbalist Nicholas Culpeper, noting its coloring properties, suggested its use as a hair dye. Thomas Chatterton mentions these "dye-berries" when writing about autumn in his *Aella* (c. 1769).

The berry's healthy virtues were extolled by an English mother who wrote in 1826 that she felt her family's excellent health was due to a little butter and plenty of blackberry preserves and treacle (presumably not at the same time).

Mythological    In Greek legend, the mortal Bellerophon dares to attempt to ride the winged horse
Pegasus to Olympus, home of the gods. He falls, landing in a thorny bush (usually taken
as being a bramble), which blinds and maims him, and he spends what remains of his
life a shunned outcast, spurned for trying to usurp the powers of the gods. Thus the
fruit symbolizes arrogance.

## Symbolic Uses of the Blackberry

- Recalling reputation as fruit of ill omen, appropriate for audit; divorce; Halloween; (on a humorous note) mother-in-law's birthday; Mother-in-Law's Day; Over-the-Hill (40th) birthday

- Recalling Shakespeare's obstinate character, appropriate for teen birthday

- Recalling the man who lost and regained his eyesight, appropriate for feast day of St. Lucy, invoked against eye ailments

- Recalling general symbolism of sorrow, appropriate for anniversary of loss; birthday of departed; farewell; funeral; Good Friday; Holocaust Memorial Day; Lent; loss; remembering departed; requiem; separation

- Recalling Creek Indian name for June, appropriate for Midsummer's Day; Midsummer's Eve; summer solstice

- Recalling symbolism of remorse, appropriate for feast day of St. Mary Magdalen

# Cherry

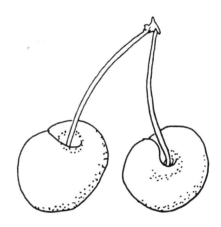

Cherries, like many fruits, appear to have originated in the Orient, possibly in China. The Romans claimed that the fruit had come to them from Cerasus in present-day Turkey, and this tradition is reflected in the botanical name of the wild or sour cherry, *Prunus cerasus* ("**plum** [of] Cerasus"). The sweet cherry is *Prunus avium*, ("**plum** [of the] birds"). The cherry's common name is derived from the Latin *cerasus*, meaning "cherry" or "cherry tree."

**Buddhist**   Maya gave birth to the Buddha as she clung to a cherry tree for support (see also **date, olive, plum**). According to one legend, the tree, recognizing the sanctity of the child, bent over and offered its fruit. This incident is said to have inspired the beautiful *Cherry Tree Carol* (see Christian). It has, however, been pointed out that similar stories about cherry trees are told in a number of cultures, including the ancient Egyptian, which told it in hieroglyphs.

Appropriately, Buddha's birthday is celebrated in Japan on April 8, when the cherries are in bloom, and indeed, some say the date marks the start of the cherry blossom season. Cherry flowers are among those used to decorate miniature temples set up to temporarily house statues of the baby Buddha, over whose image the faithful pour sweet tea in a ritual called Kam-Butsu-e, (loosely, "Buddha-bathing ceremony").

**Christian**   According to the *Cherry Tree Carol*, the pregnant Mary is out walking with Joseph and asks him to pick her some cherries. Uncharacteristically, he refuses, adding that the father of the child should get them, whereupon the tree bends down and deposits its fruit in Mary's hands. In some versions, it is the unborn child who commands the fruit tree to do so, and a French legend has a similar story substituting **apples** for cherries. This story was a popular theme for medieval Mystery Plays, which enacted biblical incidents and pious legends with equal gusto, and the carol appears to have sprung from these homely dramas.

In Christian art, cherries have other connections with Mary, for their lovely blossoms represent her purity, a symbolism echoed by the fruit itself. This was used by Titian in his *Madonna of the Cherries* (early 1500s) and the cherry is among symbolic fruit in

Joos van Cleve's *Virgin and Child with St. Joseph* (c. 1513).* (See also **pomegranate, walnut**). The fruit can also represent charity.

The cherry, as a fruit of the Tree of Paradise, also represented the happiness of those who dwelt there (see also **apple, peach, plum**).

Cherries are one of four fruits mentioned in a children's begging song sung door to door on All Souls Day, the other three being **apple, pear**, and **plum**.

It is an old custom to bring a branch of the cherry tree indoors on St. Barbara's Day so that this "Barbara Branch" will flower in time for Christmas.

Because of their religious imagery, potted cherry trees were popular as early Christmas decorations in Europe.

## Ethnic

It was formerly the custom in the winemaking area around Lower Konz, Germany, to roll a blazing "sun wheel" downhill on St. John's Eve as a charm for a good harvest. The mayor in charge of the event was always paid with a small basket of cherries.

Cherries can symbolize reconciliation, from an incident in Germany in 1432, when the children of besieged Hamburg emerged from the city, whereupon the opposing army gave them cherries from surrounding orchards, an event commemorated annually for many years.

In parts of southern Belgium, orchards were visited on the first two Sundays in Lent, when flaming torches were waved around the branches of cherry, **apple**, and **pear** trees, with pleas for a good crop of fruit from all.

---

* For other Marian symbolism, see **almond, apple, lemon, olive, raspberry, strawberry**.

Cherry Sunday was a popular summer festival in East Anglia, England. Such were its attractions that the headmaster of a boys' school in Ely recorded in 1865 that he had to caution several boys who had skipped lessons to attend the festivities about their conduct.

To the Victorians, cherry trees symbolized education, but the white cherry signified deceit.

Cherry broth was a winter staple in parts of France.

Although the national flower of Japan is the chrysanthemum, cherry blossoms symbolize spring (see also **almond, chestnut, peach, pomegranate**) and gave the country its old name, Land of the Cherry Blossoms. The blossom's popularity among the Japanese has earned it the nickname Flower of the People; in the Japanese floral calendar, April is represented by the cherry blossom (see also **peach, pear, plum**). The famous cherry trees around the Tidal Basin in Washington, D.C., were the gift of the people of Japan in 1912.

Japanese print woodblocks were made from cherry wood, and it was the custom for wood engravers to hold memorial services for the spirits of the cherry trees whose wood was used for making blocks.

In Oriental thought, the cherry blossom symbolizes feminine beauty (see also **almond, peach, plum**).

Cherry pie is a culinary icon in America, so cherries can symbolize this country (see also **apple, cranberry**).

In America, National Cherry Month is February. Washington's birthday falls that month, and the red fruit is also considered appropriate for St. Valentine's Day.

## Literary/Artistic

A story in the Finnish poem-epic collection *The Kalevala* (loosely, "Kaleva's home"), tells of Marjatta ("Berry"), a maiden who bears a child after picking (or, in some translations, eating) a berry, usually taken to be a cherry. Rejected by her family, Marjatta gives birth to a son in a stable; he grows up to be a king. The parallels with the Nativity have led to speculation that the Finnish story, originally about pagan gods, shows Christian influence at work.

In America, the fruit symbolizes honesty, from the well-known story of young George Washington's confession that he had chopped down his father's cherry tree. Ironically, the story is apocryphal, its wide currency apparently due to its appearance in the 1800 edition of Mason Locke Weems' biography of the president. In Grant Wood's painting of "Parson Weems' Fable" (1939), Weems appears as an onlooker to the alleged incident.

In poetic use, cherries have long been a symbol for beauty, especially of the mouth.

According to an old rhyme, a heavy crop of the fruit meant a merry, that is, good-omened, year ahead.

Because of its short flowering and fruiting seasons, the cherry gave its name to "Cherry Fairs," originally riotous gatherings but later referring to the transience of life as well as its pleasures. There was a nineteenth-century saying to the effect that if a woman or a cherry were painted, they both risked harm. To be "cherry merry" was to be intoxicated, perhaps on "cherry bounce" (brandy). Something of little value was "not worth a cherry stone," or a cherry, or even two bites at one (see also **fig, gooseberry, pear, persimmon**).

**Medicinal**     William Langham, in *The Garden of Health* (1579), recommended sour black cherries to "strengthen the stomak," and the fruit is a main ingredient in a Native American cure for indigestion. Bark tea from the tree was recommended for throat problems and for calming coughs, while cherry tea was given to women in labor (see also **raspberry**). Black cherry roots were used in a tonic preparation.

**Mythological**     In Greek legend, Circe the Enchantress turns Odysseus' sailors into swine, which she feeds on acorns and cornel cherries.* Odysseus escapes the same fate because he has a protective charm, a white flower given to him by Hermes, messenger of the gods (see also **hazel**). He becomes Circe's lover and persuades her to restore his men to their proper shapes.

---

\* The cornel cherry belongs to the dogwood family; in ancient times its wood was valued for weapons because of its strength.

## Symbolic Uses of the Cherry

- Recalling cherry pie as cultural icon in America, appropriate for Election Day; Flag Day; Independence Day; Lincoln's birthday; new citizen; Presidents' Day; Washington's birthday

- Recalling Victorian symbolism of education, appropriate for beginning kindergarten/college/school; commencement; graduation

- Recalling Marian symbolism, appropriate for Christmas; Epiphany; Marian festivals

- Recalling Japanese symbolism of spring, appropriate for Groundhog Day; Rogation Days; spring equinox

- Recalling begging song, appropriate for All Souls Day

- Recalling connection with birth, appropriate for adoption; birth; family/general birthdays; welcome new baby; also appropriate for feast days of Sts. Anne, patron of women in labor, and Raymond Nonnatus, patron of expectant mothers and midwives

- Recalling connection with George Washington, the "Father of His Country," appropriate for father's birthday; Father's Day; father-in-law's birthday; grandfather's birthday; Grandparent's Day

- Recalling rhyme's connection of cherries with good omens, appropriate for good fortune; groundbreaking; new job; new venture; reaching adulthood

- Recalling Barbara Branch, appropriate for St. Barbara's Day

- Recalling German reconciliation, appropriate for negotiation; peace celebration; reconciliation

- Recalling symbolism of charity, appropriate for fundraiser

- Recalling Cherry Fair's meaning of transience of life, appropriate for birthday of departed; celebration of life; funeral; Memorial Day; remembering departed; requiem; Veterans' Day; wake

## Symbolic Uses of the White Cherry

- Recalling Victorian symbolism of deceit, appropriate for audit; divorce; separation

# Citron

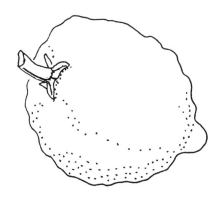

The citron (a name once used of the **lemon**) was the first citrus fruit cultivated in Europe, arriving centuries before the others. It probably originated in Asia, as many fruits did, but the Romans called it the "Median **Apple**" because it was said to have arrived in Rome from Media (in present-day northern Iran) about the first century C.E. Its botanical name, *Citrus medica* ("Citron tree [of] Media"), reflects this tradition. Later, "citrus" came to be extended to a wider range of fruits, encompassing the **grapefruit, lemon, orange**, and so on. Its common name is derived from *citrus*, ("citron tree").

**Buddhist**    In Buddhist art, a fingered citron (a type with stubby protuberances somewhat resembling fingers) is sometimes used to symbolize Buddha's hand, which in turn means protection. A folktale relates that the Buddha had cursed the fruit for its bitterness but immediately regretted his hasty words and so transformed the fruit into the shape of his hand.

**Ethnic**    According to a 1562 English herbal, citrons "fruite (at) all tymes of the year"; thus it symbolizes the harvest.

The Santal of India refer to an accidental pregnancy as the citron fruit having fallen.

In Japan, during celebrations of Toji ("winter solstice"), it is customary, especially in rural areas, to place citron halves in the bathwater, a practice thought to remove evil influence, and to eat **pumpkins** for good fortune.*

The Chinese use bowls of fragrant citrons to freshen and scent their houses.

To the Romans, citrons represented love and fidelity, so the fruit was often used as a wedding decoration.

**Judaic**    The etrog, representing the goodly fruit (Leviticus 23:40), is a citron, which customarily must be from an ungrafted tree. It is carried with the *lulav* (Hebrew, "shoot"), a bundle of **date** palm, willow, and myrtle twigs, at the Festival of Booths (also called the Festival of Tabernacles). *Succoth* is an ingathering celebration (Leviticus 23:39) and also commemorates the wanderings of the Children of Israel (Leviticus 23:42-43). Some

---

* Other observances of Toji include religious services and the lighting of bonfires.

interpret the etrog as representing both knowledge and good deeds. The booths, which give the festival its name, are rough shelters recalling temporary dwellings erected in the wilderness. By tradition, the sky should be visible through the roof, and meals are taken inside the booth, which is often decorated with flowers and fruit. (See also **fig** for a celebration involving similar shelters.)

The Talmud (Hebrew, "study," "learning") contains numerous folk remedies, among them an antidote to poisoned water: roasting and eating a honey-filled citron.

## Symbolic Uses of the Citron

- Recalling Succoth symbolism of the harvest, appropriate for harvest festival; Kwanzaa; Thanksgiving

- Recalling Japanese custom, appropriate for winter solstice

- Recalling use during the Festival of Booths and thus connections with the end of wandering, appropriate for welcome home; also appropriate for feast days of Sts. Christopher and Raphael, patrons of travelers

- Recalling Buddhist symbolism of protection, appropriate for adoption; birth

- Recalling Roman symbolism of love/fidelity, appropriate for remarriage; wedding; wedding anniversary

# Cranberry

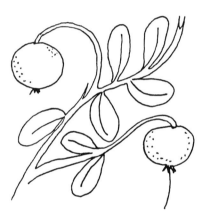

During the sixteenth and seventeenth centuries, European gourmets knew the cranberry as "fenberries" or "marshworts," after the boggy habitat in which the plant flourishes. Its common name has been derived from a folktale that the crane enjoyed them. The fruit is native to both Old and New Worlds. It belongs to the genus *Vaccinium*, "blueberry."

Ethnic

Although in America the cranberry is always connected with Thanksgiving, it seems that they were not eaten at the first such celebration in 1621, although wild **plums** and **grapes** were on the menu. Because of its connection with Thanksgiving, the cranberry represents the earth's abundance. In contemporary America, the use of strings of the berry as a Christmas ornament carries on a nineteenth-century tradition.

Germans know the berry as *moosebeere* ("moss berry") or *kronsbeere* ("crown berry").

In England, cranberries were a popular garnish for venison, a dish which could only be legally enjoyed by the upper classes. The poor, however, made cranberry preserves and doubtless enjoyed them with poached venison when available. It is, therefore, probably the most democratic fruit, with an excellent and appropriate claim to being emblematic of America (see also **apple, cherry**). In the Victorian flower language, the cranberry blossom carried a plea for the recipient to be kind to the giver.

Literary/Artistic

D.H. Lawrence's poem *Sinners* (1928) mentions the poet and a companion sitting among bushes bearing the fruit.

## Symbolic Uses of the Cranberry

- Recalling popularity as a Christmas ornament, appropriate for Christmas

- Recalling symbolism of abundance, appropriate for Earth Day; harvest festival; Kwanzaa; Thanksgiving

- Recalling folktale about crane, appropriate for feast day of St. Francis, patron of animals

- Recalling fruit's use as emblem of America, appropriate for Columbus Day; Flag Day; Independence Day; new citizen; Presidents' Day

# Date

The botanical name of the date, *Phoenix dactylifera*, is partly derived from *daktylos* (Greek, "finger"), from the shape of its foliage. "Phoenix" refers not only to the legendary bird that periodically immolated itself on a pyre (which, according to Pliny, was made of palm branches) but also means, in Phoenician, "darkish red" or "purple." Thus the botanical name for the date may be translated "darkish-red finger(like)," an apt description of the fruit. Its common name is derived from the Greek *daktylos*. The date palm is thought to have originated in the North African area.

**Christian**    Biblical references to the palm refer to the date, branches of which the crowd waved during Christ's triumphal entry into Jerusalem (Matthew 21:8-9; Mark 11:8-10; John 12:13). Appropriately, in Christian art, palm branches represent spiritual victory, justice, and righteousness; martyr-saints are often shown carrying them (see Judaic).

A late European legend (possibly inspired by the Koran; see Islamic) states that Mary bore her child under a date palm, and for this reason new mothers were once given three dates—a number also emblematic of the Trinity (see also **banana, coconut, orange**). This legend echoes the story of the birth of Apollo and Artemis (see Mythological; see also **cherry, olive, plum**).

Another story connecting Mary with dates appears in the medieval compilation *The Miracles of Mary,* which, as *Ta'Amra Maryam,* is still of importance to the Ethiopian church today. In this tale, three men are out fishing, but their boat founders and they fall into the river. Two of them call upon Mary and are saved, but the third does not and is eaten by a crocodile. The grateful survivors make a thank-offering of dates and a camel at Mary's shrine.

A legend concerning St. Christopher, patron of travelers, relates that he planted his staff in the ground, whereupon it grew into a fine date palm bearing many fruits. This story echoes both that of Aaron's rod (see Numbers 17; see also **almond**) and that of Joseph of Arimathea, who according to British legend planted his staff in the ground of Glastonbury Abbey, Somerset, where it rooted and became the Holy Thorn. Apparently a type of hawthorn, it flowered at Christmas. The bush now in the abbey ruins is said to be descended from a cutting of the original Thorn, which was uprooted by the Puritans.

One old legend has it that the date palm was formed from the spare earth which remained after Adam was created.

**Ethnic**   One of the date's earliest ritual appearances is in rock-paintings at Ouan Derbaouen in the Sahara, dating from about 1,000 B.C.E. Oxen are being driven through a U-shape of palm branches, a rite which has been interpreted as protective magic akin to the European practice of leading livestock between Midsummer and Beltane fires in order to protect them from sickness and, in particular, witchcraft. It may also have been intended to increase the herd, for dates have from ancient times been regarded as particularly potent symbols of fertility, birth, and, by extension, abundance and prosperity.

A tenth-century Arabian account tells of a pagan mid-July mourning festival in Syria, Tâ-uz. During this festival, women's meals were confined to dates, **raisins** (see **grape**), wheat, and the like, but nothing made of ground cereal could be eaten. This strongly suggests that the festival was connected with mourning for Tammuz, god of vegetation, whose annual death and resurrection was celebrated widely in the Mideast and has echoes in European folklore.[*]

One West African coastal tribe formerly tied date leaves around the trunks of sacred trees to declare their sanctity; no one could cut down or harm these trees in any way under pain of severe penalties.

Dates reportedly did not reach Europe until brought back by crusaders, but when they arrived, they received a wide welcome.

The fruit had, of course, a strong connection with the East and, by extension, to the Magi, which may account for its long popularity as a Christmas treat in Europe.

---

[*] In the Hebrew calendar, Tammuz is the month falling in June/July.

Today, a curious blend of pagan and Christian beliefs exists in some rural areas of Europe, where ashes from the Palm Sunday branches are mixed with seed corn before planting. This is said to ensure a good harvest.

Palm Donkey processions, in which the beast carried a lifesize statue of Christ, were once a feature of European Palm Sunday celebrations, and the custom is still observed in some places.

In Taoist thought, dates represented offspring.

**Persimmons** were once known as "Virginian date **plums**" or "Indian dates." The English occasionally referred to yew trees as palms, a curious inversion of the palm's symbolism of spiritual rebirth, since yews are connected with death and are common in British churchyards. Perhaps the intent was to underline that, though the body dies, the soul lives on.

Because of the palm's shape, the date has been interpreted as a masculine symbol (see also **banana, fig**).

## Hindu

Dates and **tomatoes** were among foods yogis considered to exert a calming effect upon the body, especially to the mental processes.

**Islamic**  Al-Qur'an (Arabic, "The Reading") declares that dates, **grapes**, and **olives**, being (like everything) Allah's work, are things upon which believers should ponder (Surah XIII, *Ar-Ra'd* ("The Thunder"), v. 4; Surah XVI, *An-Nahl* ("The Bee"), vv 11, 67). The date and **grape** are also mentioned in Surah XVI, v. 67, as providing food and drink; Muslims were later prohibited wine, although it will be available in Paradise (Surah XLVII, *Muhammed,** v. 15). Surah LXIX, *Al-Haggah* ("The Reality"), v. 7, describes destructive winds sent against enemies by Allah for seven days and eight nights, which left them like blown-down hollow palm trees. Surah XIX, *Maryam* ("Mary"), vv. 23-26, describes how Mary's labor pains caused her to cling to a palm, and she is consoled by its dates and water from a rivulet (see Christian).

**Judaic**  The honey mentioned in descriptions of the Promised Land is thought to be date honey rather than bee honey. Psalms 92:12 likens the flourishing of the righteous to that of the palm (see Christian). Carvings of palm trees were among the decorations of the Temple in Jerusalem (I Kings 6:29). Joel 1:7, 12 characterizes the desolated Israel as having fruitless date palms, **apple, fig**, and **pomegranate** trees, and dried-up **grape**vines.

It has been suggested that Passover foods originally included dates and **raisins** (see **grape**), which represented Egypt. Sephardic Jews include chopped dates in the Passover haroset because the fruit gives the mixture a more mortar-like appearance (see **apple**).

---

\* Named after the prophet, who is mentioned in verse 2.

Dates are praised in the Talmud as being warming, strengthening, and satisfying, with the caveat that they are harmful if eaten at certain times, though without compare if consumed at midday.

Dates are part of numerous folk remedies mentioned in the Talmud, for example in cures for intestinal worms (eat a half-ripened white date [see also **blackberry**]) and for skin eruptions (soak the feet in two bowls of water in which date stones and cedar leaves respectively have been boiled\*). Date water was also to be rubbed on children with hornet stings, the remainder being drunk to complete the cure. Fits of periodic fever such as malaria were to be treated by a mixture of palm tree prickles, dirt, pitch and such tied in a bag to the shirt. Bleeding could be stanched by applying vinegar in which dates had been steeped.

Palm branches form part of the *lulav* carried during Succoth (see **citron**).

Moroccan Jews celebrate the end of Passover with a buffet meal which includes yeastcakes and dates.

## Mythological

In an inscription from Ur, the king refers to himself as a date palm growing by water. (The date palm was the Tree of Life in Mesopotamian mythology.) In their art and sculpture, the king was often depicted tending palms so that, through his labors, the nation would receive all manner of divine blessings.

Dates were also sacred to the great Egyptian goddess Isis and to Greek Artemis (Roman Diana). Artemis, a virginal deity, was goddess of the hunt and childbirth. Her second

---

\* The cedar water may then be drunk, but not the date water because this was said to cause sterility, which is rather curious in view of the fertility generally ascribed to the fruit.

role is derived from the story of her mother Leto (Lato or Latona), who became pregnant by Zeus and thus was in ill favor with Zeus' wife, Hera. Hera ordered that Leto could not give birth on land or sea or in any place upon which sunlight had fallen. Hunted and harried from place to place, Leto finally gave birth clinging for support to a palm tree (in some versions, a palm and an **olive**) on a newly risen island provided by Poseidon, god of the sea, who held a wave over it to block the sun (see also **cherry, plum**). Leto bore twins—Artemis, who, newly born, assisted her mother with the birth of Apollo. It has been suggested that the famous many-breasted statue of Diana at Ephesus (whose worship is mentioned in Acts 19) was, in fact, Artemis/Diana, covered from neck to waist with sacred dates. Lucian records seeing a date palm growing from an altar to Apollo, which was therefore accorded much honor by devotees of the god.

## Literary/Artistic

Palms, as well as laurels, were awarded to victorious Greek generals, and an echo of this is found in the name of Palmerin de Oliva, hero of sixteenth-century Spanish legends. De Oliva took his name from the grove of date palms and **olive** trees in which his mother—supposedly of royal blood—abandoned him.

The "palmers" or "palmerers" mentioned in Shakespeare's *Romeo and Juliet* (1597) and in the prologue of Chaucer's *Canterbury Tales* (written between 1386 and 1400) were itinerant "professional" pilgrims.

## Symbolic Uses of the Date

- Recalling symbolism of abundance, appropriate for Earth Day; harvest festival; Kwanzaa; Thanksgiving

- Recalling symbolism of the Trinity, appropriate for Trinity Sunday

- Recalling Christian symbolism of spiritual victory, appropriate for All Saints Day; All Souls Day; baptism; celebration of life; Easter Sunday; funeral; pilgrimage; saints' feast days (particularly martyrs'); wake

- Recalling Christ's entry into Jerusalem, appropriate for Palm Sunday

- Recalling Christian symbolism of justice, appropriate for Election Day; jury duty; taking office; also appropriate for feast day of St. Yves, patron of lawyers

- Recalling legend about St. Christopher's staff, appropriate for his feast day

- Recalling twin symbolisms of martyrdom and righteousness, appropriate for Martin Luther King, Jr., Day

- Recalling symbolism of fertility, appropriate for baby shower; birth; welcome new baby

- Recalling symbolism of masculinity, boy's birthday; men's festivals

- Recalling palms of victory, appropriate for long service award; milestones; premiere; promotion; reaching adulthood; reaching goal; recognition award; sports victory

- Recalling connection with the Magi, appropriate for Christmas; Epiphany

- Recalling folk remedy mentioned in the Talmud, appropriate for feast day of St. Domitian, invoked against fever

- Recalling yogis' belief, appropriate for religious retreat

# *Elderberry*

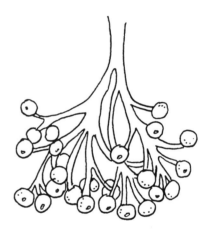

Like the **blackberry**, the elderberry is a fruit of ill omen. The elderberry belongs to the genus *Sambucus*, derived from the Latin *sambuca*, a harp-like instrument traditionally made from elderwood. Native to both Old and New Worlds, its common name is derived from the High German *holander* ("hollow"), referring to its twigs (see note on "bour tree" in Ethnic entry).

**Christian**  Central European tradition claims that the Cross was made of elderwood, and an old rhyme states that, because of this, the elder tree will always be small, crooked, and feeble. It is said that Judas hanged himself upon an elder tree (see also **fig**.) Elderberries therefore symbolize sorrow and remorse (see also **blackberry, raspberry**).

**Ethnic**  Humankind's brief lifespan is explained by a Native American legend of the Tsimschian of the northwest American coast. The elderberry won an argument with a boulder as to which would give birth to humankind during the dawn of the world. Had the boulder won, people would have had a longer lifespan rather than dying after a relatively short time.

In the Victorian flower language, a branch of elder meant remorse (see also **blackberry, raspberry**). The elder blossom represented sorrow, although it could also symbolize zeal. Like the **blackberry** and the **pear**, the elderberry was considered a "fairy" tree, and making a cradle from its wood was very unwise, for any child rocked in it would never thrive.*

British folklore claims that badgers prefer elder trees above all others as scratching posts.

An old name for the elderberry was "bour tree" or "bore tree," from the use of its hollowed-out twigs for children's toys such as whistles and blowguns (see introductory statement to this section).

---

* Better choices were said to be **hazel** or birch.

**Literary/Artistic**   In his reconstructed Druid Tree Alphabet, Robert Graves makes the elderberry the tree of the unlucky thirteenth month, beginning November 25 and representing the letter "R" (see also **blackberry, grape, hazel**).

Bearing in mind the fruit's generally bad reputation, there is some justice in the choice of elderberry wine as the means of disposing of boarders in Joseph Kesselring's *Arsenic and Old Lace* (1941).

In the sixteenth century, "Your Elderberryness" was used as a mock title or to poke fun at someone (see also **pumpkin**).

**Medicinal**   Elder flowers make a refreshing tea. Country folk mixed elder leaves and tansy as a fly repellent (see also **walnut**). Elder-leaf collars, ironically in view of the Judas legend (see Christian), were considered panaceas for neck problems.

**Mythological**   In pagan mythology, all trees were inhabited by spirits, and those of the elderberry were particularly vindictive. Thus, to destroy an elder tree was to invite all manner of trouble, while burning elderwood would bring evil to a dwelling. A Cornish variant from England has it that burning elder logs would bring Lucifer to sit on the chimney. Sleeping under an elder tree brought dreams of death.

## Symbolic Uses of the Elderberry

- Recalling connection with harp, appropriate for feast day of St. Cecilia, patron of musicians

- Recalling use for children's toys, appropriate for children's birthdays; Children's Day

- Recalling symbolism of zeal, appropriate for dedication; pilgrimage; Secretaries' Day; sports victories; taking office

- Recalling reputation as fruit of ill omen, appropriate for audit; Halloween; (on a humorous note) mother-in-law's birthday; Mother-in-Law's Day; Over-the-Hill (40th) birthday

- Recalling use of "Your Elderberryness" to poke fun, appropriate for April Fool's Day

- Recalling symbolism of remorse, appropriate for feast day of St. Mary Magdalen

- Recalling folktale about badgers, appropriate for feast day of St. Francis, patron of animals

- Recalling symbolism of sorrow, appropriate for anniversary of loss; birthday of departed; divorce; farewell; funeral; Good Friday; Holocaust Memorial Day; Lent; loss; remembering departed; requiem; separation; wake

# *Fig*

The fig's botanical name, *Ficus carica* ("fig tree [of] Caria"), recalls its supposed origins in that country, now part of Turkey. It appears to have originated in the Mediterranean area, and its common name is derived from the Middle English "fige" via the Old English "fic," from *ficus*. Figs have been cultivated for over five thousand years and play a major role in many religions and legends.

**Buddhist**     The *bo* tree under which Buddha reached enlightenment was a type of fig, the *pipal* or *Ficus religiosa* ("sacred [or holy] fig tree"). *Bo* tree is derived from the Sanskrit *bodhi-taru*, "knowledge tree," with a sense of "achieving awareness" or "reaching perfect understanding" (see Hindu).

The fig symbolizes contemplation, enlightenment, and rejection of bodily temptation. It was once used in Buddhist art as a symbol of Buddha, actual likenesses of whom were not generally painted for almost five hundred years after his death. Such is the sanctity of the *bo* tree that, it is said, a devout Buddhist will not tell lies in its shadow.

**Christian**     Figs are the first fruit mentioned by name in the Bible (Genesis 3:7). Adam and Eve fashion "aprons" from its leaves when they become aware of, and ashamed about, their nakedness. Figs have therefore been suggested as the fruit of Tree of Knowledge (see also **apple, banana, lemon, orange, pomegranate, quince, tomato**).

The Holy Family is said to have rested under a fig tree during the Flight to Egypt (see also **peach**).

Luke 6:44 mentions the fig in a parable pointing out that people are known by their works (see also **blackberry, grape**). Matthew 7:15-16 uses similar phrasing when warning against false prophets.

Luke 13:6-9 relates the parable of the fig tree that has not borne fruit in three years. Its owner orders its destruction, but the husbandman pleads for another year of grace for the tree. This has been interpreted as meaning that there was still time for Israel to repent. The blasting of the barren fig tree noted in Mark 11:12-14 and Matthew 21:18-19 may refer to this. Both chapters draw a parallel between the fig's destruction and the power of faith.*

Luke 21:29-31 and Matthew 24:32-33 note, just as the greening of figs and other trees foretells summer (see also **plum**), so certain signs mean that the Kingdom of God is near.

John 1:48 notes that the guileless (v. 47) Nathanael was seen by Jesus under a fig tree, before Philip arrived to ask the former to go and see Jesus.

According to Sicilian legend, Judas hanged himself upon a fig tree (see also **elderberry**).

Ethnic Childless Roman women used fig sap as a fertility charm (see also **coconut, orange, pomegranate**).

Because of its masculine symbolism, the **banana** was once called "Adam's fig, " and a particular type growing in the Indies is known as the fig-**banana** (see also **date**).

In a scapegoat ritual practiced by early Greeks, human victims ate cheese, barley loaves, and figs before being beaten with branches of fig and other sacred trees—intended as a purifying measure—and subsequently sacrificed. During Thargelia, a May festival, strings

---

* It has been suggested that the fig tree's destruction may be a symbolic rejection of pagan religion, in particular that of the Earth or Mother Goddess to whom the fig, as a symbol of the yoni (female genitalia), was especially sacred. See Walker, *Woman's Encyclopedia*, 1983.

of figs were hung around the necks of two scapegoats (also occasionally human) before they were banished or, in some cases, stoned to death, thus removing communal sins. Thargelia may also have been connected with the fig harvest; its name has been associated with "first fruits."

Villagers on the island of Rhodes hang marjoram on their fig trees on St. Constantine's Day. This is considered to betroth the tree to its owner, and it is said that unless the custom is carried out annually the trees will not bear fruit, thinking their "betrothed" to be dead.

Figs, like **grapes** and **olives**, were sacred in Crete.

Palm Sunday was once known as Fig Sunday in England, recalling the blasting of the barren fig tree (see Christian). Fig Sue, a dish made of figs boiled in ale with pieces of bread, was eaten on the day in commemoration of the event.

Carrying on an Aztec tradition, paper-makers in the San Pablito, Mexico, area use the boiled bark of the wild fig to make paper needed for ritual purposes such as healing and love-charms.

In general, like the **blackberry** and **tomato**, figs represent lust.

## Hindu

Agni was god of fire in all its manifestations, including comets, lightning, and the bodily passions. A legend concerning him relates that he was pursued by the other gods and tried to elude them by hiding in various places. He hid underwater but was betrayed by a toad; he concealed himself in an *asvattha* (*Ficus religiosa* [see Buddhist]) but an elephant revealed his whereabouts; he hid in a stick of bamboo but a parrot pointed him out to his pursuers. Agni cursed all three, which is why toads croak, elephants eat with their noses, and parrots cannot talk properly. Finally Agni took up residence in a *sami* tree, which henceforth was regarded as the home of fire. Its wood is used for sacred blazes, and the crackling of flames is regarded as Agni's voice (see also **hazel, pear**).

In Hindu art, Visnu is sometimes shown as, or above, a fig tree; he was said to have been born under one.

Fig trees were regarded as Trees of Knowledge and virtually sentient in their own right.

## Islamic

The Prophet swore by both fig and **olive** (Al Qur'an, Surah XCV, *At-Tin* ["The Fig"], v. 1).

## Judaic

In Judges 9:8-15 the fig refuses Kingship of the Trees on account of its sweetness in a parable relating to an upstart claimant to the throne (see also **blackberry, grape**vine, **olive**).

Figs and **raisins** (see **grape**) are among foods at David's coronation (I Chronicles 12:40) and both are among gifts brought by Abigail on her mission of peace (I Samuel 25:18).

Figs, like the **grape**vine, **olive**, and **pomegranate**, grow in the Promised Land (Deuteronomy 8:8). Its desolation is characterized as having fruitless fig trees and **grape**vines, and withered **apple** and **pomegranate** trees and **date** palms (Joel 1:7, 12).

Jeremiah 8:13 states that when judgment comes, fig trees and **grape**vines will be bare.

Figs are mentioned with **grape**vines in connection with the days of peace and plenty, when people will live in harmony together (Micah 4:4; Zechariah 3:10).

Strongholds ready to be conquered are likened to figs, which will fall when the tree is shaken (Nahum 3:12).

Proverbs 27:18 notes that the fig tree's keeper eats of its fruit; that is, the servant, too, will gain honor.

Jeremiah 24 relates a vision of two baskets, one filled with delicious figs, the other filled with inedible figs. The "good" figs are the captive Jews in exile, who will all be saved; the "bad" figs are King Zedekiah and his minions, who will all be consumed and destroyed.

In contemporary Israel, figs are eaten with **almonds, grapes, olives**, and **pomegranates** during Tu Bi-Shevat (for more on this festival, see **olive**).

## Literary/Artistic

The Latino obscene gesture known as "making the fig" is mentioned in Shakespeare's *Henry VI, Part II* (1594) and *The Merry Wives of Windsor* (1602).

The colloquialism "not giving a fig" is a bowdlerized version of the message of the gesture, while "not worth a fig," meaning of little or no value, has been in use since the early 1600s (see also **cherry, gooseberry, pear, persimmon**). This usage may be why counterfeiters referred to their handiwork as "figs."

The "Italian fig" or "Spanish fig" could be either the gesture mentioned or the poisoned fruit (apparently of any kind) with which it was once the regrettable custom to dispose of one's enemies. Despite this, "ffgeye" was a popular sweetmeat in the Middle Ages. It was often tri-colored red, yellow, and brown; one of its earliest appearances is in a cookbook dating from the 1400s. The "figgy pudding" mentioned in the traditional carol "We Wish You A Merry Christmas," however, is one made of **raisins** (see **grape**).

A character in Charles Dickens' *Dombey and Son* (1847-8) remarks that one should guide a fig tree in its growth so as to be able to enjoy its shade when old, a comment recalling the advice on raising children in Proverbs 22:6.

In classical art and statuary, the genitals were covered with fig leaves.

"Full fig" (from "full figure") means to dress up with all the trimmings; hence "figgery" for ostentatious decoration on one's garments; "figging out" or "up," meaning to equip or smarten up; and the related "figging," picking pockets.

## Mythological

In Babylonian art, the goddess Ishtar was sometimes represented by a fig tree with roots in the underworld and branches in the heavens.

According to a Babylonian legend, when Creation was complete, the worm supplicated the sun god Shamash for food. Offered figs and **apricots,** it rejected both in favor of taking up residence in the teeth and gums, thus becoming the ancestor of toothaches (see also **olive, walnut**). Appropriately, Germans chewed figs as a toothache cure.

The Persian sun god Mithras, born at the winter solstice, was "adopted" by a fig tree; that is, he used its leaves for clothing and ate its fruit (see also **grape**).

Herodotus records that when bulls were sacrificed to Egyptian gods, the animals were slaughtered, their carcasses filled with herbs, myrrh, honey, figs, and **raisins** (see **grape**) and burnt.

A fig tree in the Forum at Rome was said to have been sacred to Romulus, co-founder of the city, and was thus accorded much honor. It may have been the same tree which, according to Roman mythology, was sacred to the Etruscan goddess Rumina, and under which Romulus and his twin Remus were nursed by the she-wolf. Roman women honored Juno, queen of heaven, at a festival on July 7, held under or near fig trees, acknowledging the fruit's role as a symbol of the yoni (female genitalia; see also **almond, apricot, grape, pomegranate**).

Hyacinthus, the beautiful youth beloved by Apollo, died by accident, and Spartans honored him at a summer festival with a feast of goat's meat, beans, cheese, and figs consumed in shelters made of branches, reminiscent of those erected for Succoth (see **citron**). Dionysus, Greek god of wine and merriment, was also patron of trees, and figs and **apples** (as well as **grapes**) were particularly sacred to him. Greek gardeners offered Priapus, god of male generative powers, figs as well as **apples, grapes, quinces**, and vegetables in order to gain his protection for their crops. Iris, goddess of the rainbow, was honored with offerings of wheatcakes, figs, and nuts. Greek mythology stated that the fig tree was given to humankind by the corn goddess, Demeter, who presented the first to Phytelus, an Athenian who gave her hospitality as she searched for her lost daughter, Persephone (see also **olive, pomegranate**).

Figs are the Tree of Life in some Oceanic cultures. They are also sacred to the Indonesian god Upu-Lera ("Mr. Sun") (see also **coconut**).

An Australian Aboriginal legend tells of a fig tree in an account of hazards faced by souls after death. The shade's journey takes it past a fig tree in which an enemy lurks. This enemy will attack the spirit by throwing clumps of figs, magically turned to stone, at it. These missiles either kill outright or inflict wounds that never heal. However, if the departed has led a good life, the shade of a relative or friend will be nearby to warn of the danger, which can thus be avoided.

Another Aboriginal legend tells of an old man who sleeps under a fig tree, dreaming of a new song and dance. On awakening, he teaches them to his two sons, who turn into cranes and fly away to teach them to the other tribes.

In Europe, fig cultivation was originally a woman's mystery, and in pagan art a basket of figs symbolized the Earth or Mother Goddess (see also **grape, pomegranate**).

## Symbolic Uses of the Fig

- Recalling pagan symbolism of Earth or Mother Goddess and thus femininity, appropriate for bridal shower; wedding; women's festivals

- Recalling Buddhist symbolism of rejection of temptation, appropriate for engagement; remarriage

- Recalling Babylonian legend, appropriate for first tooth and for feast day of St. Apollonia, invoked against toothaches

- Recalling Mithraic legend, appropriate for adoption; winter solstice

- Recalling colloquialism meaning "not caring," appropriate for divorce; separation

- Recalling Judaic connection with harmony, peace and plenty, appropriate for Earth Day; harvest festival; Kwanzaa; peace celebration; reconciliation; Thanksgiving

- Recalling role as Tree of Knowledge, appropriate for beginning kindergarten/college/school; commencement; graduation

- Recalling blasting of barren fig tree, appropriate for Palm Sunday

- Recalling Rhodes custom, appropriate for St. Constantine's Day; also for feast day of St. Fiacre, patron of gardeners

- Recalling symbolism of contemplation, appropriate for religious retreat

- Recalling role in Tu Bi-Shevat, appropriate for Arbor Day

- Recalling connections with fertility, appropriate for baby shower; birth; family/general birthday; welcome new baby

# Gooseberry

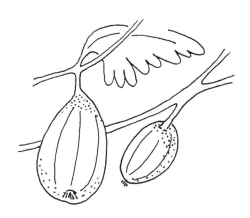

Gooseberries received their common name, it is said, from their popularity as a sauce accompanying goose, their acidic content counteracting the bird's rather fatty taste. In Europe in general, however, it is **chestnut** or **prune** (see **plum**) stuffing that accompanies the St. Martin's Day goose. Gooseberries belong to the genus *Ribes*, derived from the Arabic *ribas*, meaning "of acid taste." Gooseberries are native to both Old and New Worlds.

**Ethnic**    In parts of Transylvania, it was formerly the custom on Ascension Day for girls to dress a cornsheaf in female clothing and carry it around the village. They then withdrew indoors, removed the sheaf's clothing, and handed the sheaf to boys waiting outside, who threw it into the river. In the meantime, one of the girls donned the discarded clothing and another procession was held, culminating in a meal in her home from which boys were excluded. It was then considered safe for fruit, in particular gooseberries, to be eaten because the foregoing rituals had removed Death from them.

Gooseberry Fool was a popular medieval dessert and still has its admirers today. It is composed of a mixture of cream and sieved gooseberries, and its name is thought to derive from *fouler*, meaning, in French, "to press" (i.e., through a sieve).

British children inquiring from whence babies came were (and still are) often told that they are found "under a gooseberry bush" (rather than under a cabbage leaf as mentioned by Americans in answer to the same question). Appropriately, in the Victorian flower language, the gooseberry blossom symbolized anticipation.

**Literary/Artistic**    In newspaper parlance, the "great gooseberry season" was used of a slow period where little "real" news was available, so space was filled by well-illustrated accounts of such trivia as gooseberries of record-breaking size. In his *Sketches by Boz* (1836), Charles Dickens relates the delight of an elderly retired couple who grow such a gooseberry and display it to all their visitors. The phrase was therefore a forerunner of today's "silly season," used in the same colloquial sense. The colloquialism "playing gooseberry," meaning to be the odd one out in a trio (especially when the other two are a courting couple), was also used of someone acting as a chaperone.

"Playing old gooseberry," mentioned in Dickens' *Martin Chuzzlewit* (1843), referred to causing chaos or destruction (see also **apple**).

In criminal argot, "going gooseberrying" meant stealing clothing from washing lines.

As with **cherry, fig, pear**, and **persimmon**, the gooseberry appears in a phrase meaning something of small or no value, as in "not worth a gooseberry."

"Gooseberry fairs" were races held at the side of the road.

An archaic name for a frizzy hairpiece was "gooseberry wig," from its resemblance to a gooseberry bush.

## Symbolic Uses of the Gooseberry

- Recalling Victorian symbolism of anticipation, appropriate for adoption; Advent; baby shower; birth; bridal shower

- Recalling literary connection with causing chaos, appropriate for sports victories

- Recalling Transylvanian custom, appropriate for Ascension Day

- Recalling colloquialism for wig, appropriate for first haircut

- Recalling culinary use, appropriate for St. Martin's Day; recalling his role as patron of soldiers, appropriate for Armed Forces Day; enlistment; military discharge

- Recalling colloquialism for odd one out, appropriate for divorce; separation

- Recalling newspaper usage, appropriate for April Fool's Day

# Grape

## with notes on Raisin and Currant

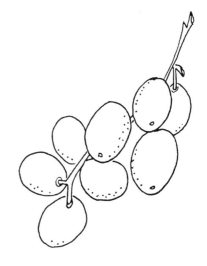

Native to both Old and New Worlds, grapes are one of the most anciently cultivated fruits. The Hittite Law Code protected them, as it did **apple** and **pomegranate** trees. Its common name is derived from the Old French *grappe*, meaning, among other things, "a bunch (or stalk) of grapes." Its botanical name, *Vitis vinifera*, means, loosely, "wine-bearing grape."

**Christian**   Luke 6:44 notes that thorns do not produce **figs**, nor brambles (**blackberries**) grapes, meaning people are known by their works. A similar phrase is used in Matthew 7:15-16 in warning against false prophets.

Matthew 21:28-32 relates the parable of two sons sent to work in their father's vineyard. One initially refuses, but works there anyway. The other agrees to go, but does not. The meaning of this parable is that obedience (as parents of teenagers know better than most) is less a matter of words than of actions.

The parable of the hiring of vineyard laborers, related in Matthew 20:1-16, is enigmatic at first glance, for the payment of the same wages to all, regardless of hours worked, seems unfair. It has, however, been interpreted to mean that God extends grace to all who labor in God's vineyard, whether they come to it early or late.

Matthew 21, Mark 12, and Luke 20 all mention the parable concerning the absentee landlord of a vineyard. The husbandmen would not render him its fruits, as the law required, so servants were sent to deal with them, but the servants are beaten and killed. The owner finally sends his son, whom the husbandmen murder, thinking they can thus keep the fruit themselves. The parable ends by stating the owner will return and destroy the miscreants, giving the vineyard to others. The story is an allegory dealing with the shabby treatment of Jesus, who had come to Israel, the Lord's vineyard (see Judaic), and of the prophets before him.

Jesus' first miracle was turning water into wine at the marriage feast at Cana (John 2:1-10).

John 15:1 records Jesus' statement that he is a vine and God is the husbandman, while we are its branches (v. 5), echoing Isaiah 5:7 (see Judaic).

The medicinal use of wine is mentioned in I Timothy 5:23, which advises drinking a little for stomach aches or other infirmities.

God's wrath is likened to a winepress (Revelation 14:19), providing the imagery used in John Steinbeck's *The Grapes of Wrath* (1939) and Julia Ward Howe's "Battle Hymn of the Republic" (1861).

In the Mass, wine symbolizes the blood of Christ and bread, his body (Matthew 26:26-28; Mark 14:22-24; Luke 22:19-20).

Sacramental vessels are often engraved with grapevines, a symbol of resurrection.

In sacred art, grapes represent sacrifice because they must be destroyed to make wine (see also **olive**).

The Tree of Jesse, showing Jesus' earthly lineage, is often depicted as a grapevine; the term is also used of a branching candlestick because of its resemblance to a tree.

## Ethnic

The first corn and grapes are offered to St. James the Greater on his feast day in Pontevedra, Spain (for other first-fruit rituals, see also **pumpkin, raspberry**).

In the winemaking area around Lower Konz, Germany, it was formerly the custom to roll blazing straw "sun-wheels" downhill on St. John's Eve to ensure a good harvest. Curiously, the mayor of such proceedings was always paid with a basket of **cherries**.

Wild grapes and **plums** were offered at the first American Thanksgiving in 1621, although apparently not **cranberries**.

Germans call the grape *weinbeere*, "wineberry."

Like the **fig** and **olive**, grapes were sacred in Crete.

**Islamic**  Al-Qur'an points to grapes, **dates**, and **olives** as, like everything, Allah's work and thus things upon which believers should ponder (Surah XIII, *Ar-Ra'd* ("The Thunder"), v. 4; Surah XVI, *An-Nahl* ("The Bee"), vv. 11, 67). The grape and **date** are also mentioned in Surah XVI, v. 67, as providing food and drink. Muslims were later prohibited wine, although it will be available in Paradise (Surah XLVII, *Muhammed*, v. 15).

**Judaic**  Israel is the Lord's vineyard (Isaiah 5:7). However, its degeneration (Jeremiah 2:21) leads to the prophecy that its enemies will go over its remains, as gleaners who search for the last grapes (Jeremiah 6:9).

Joel 1:7, 12 characterize the desolate Israel as having fruitless grapevines, **fig, apple, and pomegranate** trees and **date** palms, while Jeremiah 8:13 states that when judgment comes, neither grapes nor **figs** will bear fruit.

Noah planted a vineyard after the Flood, becoming an husbandman (Genesis 9:20).

Genesis 40 relates that Joseph interprets a dream for a fellow prisoner, in which the dreamer sees a three-branched vine bearing fruit and blossom and makes wine from the grapes for his former master, the Pharaoh. Joseph correctly states that this means that the dreamer will be restored to royal favor in three days.

The vine of Sodom has bitter grapes (Deuteronomy 32:32; see also **apple**).

Ezekiel 18:2 mentions a proverb applied to Israel, concerning fathers eating sour grapes, thus setting their children's teeth on edge. This apparently meant that Israel could not blame its forefathers for its plight, for by repentance and returning to the Lord, it could avoid inheriting their sins (see also Jeremiah 31:29-30).

Judges 9:8-15 relates a parable concerning an upstart claimant to the throne. The grapevine declines kingship of the trees on account of its role in winemaking (see also **blackberry, fig, olive**).

Grapevines, **figs, olives**, and **pomegranates** grow in the Promised Land (Deuteronomy 8:8).

Micah 4:4 and Zechariah 3:10 speak of the days of peace and plenty, when everyone will sit under their vines and **fig** trees in harmony.[*]

Psalms 128:3 compares a wife to a vine and children to **olive** trees.

Numbers 6:3-4 forbids anything from the vine, including its fruit, to Nazarites during their days of consecration to the Lord; the same instructions are given to Samson's mother before she bears her child (who is to be a lifelong Nazarite), as recorded in Judges 13:4-7.

Harvest gleanings to be left for orphans, widows, and strangers include grapes and **olives** (Deuteronomy 24:19-21).

At the beginning of the Shabbes (Hebrew, "rest," i.e., the Sabbath) meal, the *kiddush* ("sanctification") cup is filled with wine and blessed, thanking the Lord, who created grapes, for the Sabbath. A similar ritual marks Havdalah ("separation"), the conclusion of the Sabbath. A blessing is recited over wine and sweet spices are sniffed to alleviate the sadness caused by the end of the Sabbath as it is separated from the week.

---

[*] The Romans stated that it took five years to get a good vintage from a wine and an equal period for **olive** trees to bear a good crop; hence a lengthy time of peace was necessary to enjoy both.

It is customary to drink four cups of wine during the Pesach ("pass over, spare"; thus, Passover) seder ("order") meal. This number has been connected with Exodus 6:6-7, in which the Lord makes four promises to the Children of Israel: they will be delivered from Egypt, freed, redeemed and be God's chosen people. A fifth cup is poured for Elijah, and the door opened for him, for his arrival will herald the Messiah.

At Jewish weddings, the couple sips one cup of wine during the ceremony to represent their engagement, and then a second cup to represent the marriage itself.

In contemporary Israel, grapes are eaten during Tu Bi-Shevat (see also **almond, fig, olive, pomegranate**).

## Literary/Artistic

In Greek art, figures of autumn held grapevines and **olive** boughs; in pagan art in general, grapevines symbolized pleasure, revelry and abandon, as well as the sudden and unprovoked wrath of the intoxicated.

In his reconstructed Druid Tree Alphabet, Robert Graves makes the grapevine (an alternative to the native **blackberry**) the "tree" of the tenth month, beginning September 2 and representing the letter "M" (see also **elderberry, hazel**).

One of Aesop's fables tells about a fox who, having failed to get some grapes, goes away saying that they were probably sour anyway, giving us the colloquialism "sour grapes" for the dismissal of something not attainable, though much desired, as worthless.*

---

\* There are many public houses in the United Kingdom named "The Fox and the Grapes" from this story, although the name is something of a left-handed compliment.

The "grapevine telegraph" is another name for the "bush telegraph" or rapid (and apparently magical) transmission of information or rumor over long distances.

Though the **grapefruit** is not related to the grape, it is named after the way it clusters on the tree.

The military term "a whiff of grapeshot," meaning achieving victory without much action or, in some cases, merely by threatening it, has been traced to an analogy used by Thomas Carlyle in *The History of the French Revolution* (1837), where he writes about Napoleon Bonaparte's walkover victory during a Parisian uprising.

During the short-lived French revolutionary calendar, the month beginning September 22 was called Vendémiaire, "vintage."

In one version of the tragic love story of Tristan and Isolde, King Mark orders a rosebush planted on Isolde's grave and a grapevine on Tristan's. The two plants grow inseparably together, a symbol of the lovers' fidelity (see also **hazel**).

## Mythological

According to Egyptian legend, Osiris, god of resurrection, introduced the cultivation of grapes and winemaking to their nation. Some papyri show his shrine decorated with grapes (for example, that of Nebseni, c. 1500 B.C.E.) or with vines growing nearby. His followers were expected not to harm vines or any fruit tree.

Grape and ivy leaf chaplets crowned followers of Dionysus, god of wine and merriment (to whom, as patron of trees, grapes, **apples**, and **figs** were particularly sacred) and of his Roman equivalent, Bacchus or Liber. One of several Greek festivals honoring Dionysus was the Oschophoria, meaning, loosely, "carrying grape bunches." The ships of Dionysus featured in his rites recalled a legend in which he was captured by pirates, whom he routed by turning himself into a lion and causing ivy and grapevines to grow from the ship's mast. In another story, one of his followers, Ampelus, was killed climbing a tree to pick grapes from a vine growing on it, so Dionysus turned him into the constellation Vindimitor ("grape gatherer") and set him in the sky.*

In Greek legend, Tantalus was a mortal who offended the gods by stealing their ambrosia and nectar and, among other things, swearing false oaths in Zeus' name. His punishment was perpetual hunger and thirst and standing up to the neck in water, which receded when he bent to drink, with clusters of grapes and other fruit overhead, which moved away when he tried to eat (hence "tantalizing" him).

Greek gardeners offer Priapus, god of male generative powers, grapes, **apples, figs, quinces**, and vegetables in order to gain his protection for their crops.

Grapes, as a symbol of the yoni (female genitalia), also represented the Earth or Mother Goddess (see also **almond, apricot, fig, pomegranate**).

Romans celebrated the Feast of Vineyard Jupiter on August 19, and grape harvesting could not commence until one of the god's priests had sacrificed a lamb and picked the first bunch of grapes, a ritual acknowledging the sanctity of first fruits (see also **pumpkin, raspberry**).

According to Persian legend, when Mithras slew the Bull (the first created creature), the world was formed from various parts of its body. Living creatures sprang from its seed, vegetation from its blood and spine, and the grapevine from its tail (see also **fig, plum**).

---

* Another version has it that Zeus turned the youth into a grapevine.

# *Raisin*

Raisins, dried grapes, derived their name from the Latin *racemus*, meaning, loosely, "berry clusters"; in French, *raisin* refers to the grape.

**Judaic**  David's coronation feast included raisins and **figs** (I Chronicles 12:40), and Abigail brought both among gifts for him on her mission of peace (I Samuel 25:18). It has been suggested that raisins and **dates** were originally Passover foods, representing Egypt (see also **apple**).

**Ethnic**  A mid-July Syrian mourning festival, Tâ-uz, probably connected with the worship of the god of vegetation, Tammuz, permitted women the consumption of raisins, wheat, or **dates**, but not ground cereals.

Raisin pie was such a feature of colonial funerals in New England and Pennsylvania that to inquire if one was needed indicated that the patient was seriously ill.

Raisins are one of the chief ingredients in the triple-loaf Trinity Bread eaten by Greeks at Easter.

Pan de Muerto (Spanish, "bread of death"), taken to family graves with other food and gifts on Mexico's Dias de Muertos (Spanish, "day of [the] dead"), or All Souls Day, generally contains raisins.

Christmas celebrations in Victorian England often included Snapdragon, a dangerous pastime whereby raisins were snatched from a bowl of burning brandy. After numerous tragic accidents, the game fortunately fell out of favor.

**Literary/Artistic**  The **figs** in the "figgy pudding" mentioned in the popular carol "We Wish You A Merry Christmas" are, in fact, raisins ("fig" being an English dialect word for them).

In traditional symbolism, raisins, by virtue of their shriveled appearance, represent lost hopes or dreams, a reference used in Lorraine Hansberry's classic 1959 play, *A Raisin in the Sun.*

**Medicinal**  In former times, both raisins and **currants** were considered beneficial to the health, and in *The Castel of Helth* (1539), Sir Thomas Elyot wrote that "raysons do make the stomache firme and strong."

**Mythological**  Herodotus recorded that bulls offered to Egyptian gods were first slaughtered, their carcasses filled with raisins, herbs, honey, myrrh, and **figs**, and then burnt.

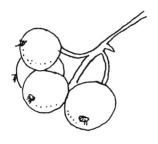

# Currant

Currants are small, seedless raisins, which derived their name from the French *raisins de Coraunts*, "grapes of Corinth," a major Greek growing area for the fruit for centuries. In addition, currants can also refer to the fruit of the black or red currant bush, which belong to the genus *Ribes*, from the Arabic *ribas*, meaning "of acid taste." They are native to both Old and New Worlds.

**Ethnic**   Victorians used currant flowers to convey the message that the recipient pleased the giver (see also **peach**).

**Medicinal**   As noted in **raisin**, currants have long been considered beneficial to the health. English herbalists recommended black currants for curing quinsy.

## Symbolic Uses of the Grape

- Recalling the eucharistic wine's symbolism of the Blood of Christ, appropriate for baptism; confirmation; first eucharist

- Recalling Christian symbolism of sacrifice, appropriate for Good Friday; Memorial Day

- Recalling role in Tu Bi-Shevat, also appropriate for Arbor Day

- Recalling Spanish and Roman customs, appropriate for first fruits

- Recalling biblical connection with abundance, appropriate for Earth Day; harvest festival; Kwanzaa; Thanksgiving

- Recalling pagan artistic symbolism of, and biblical connection with, wrath, appropriate for divorce; separation

- Recalling Spanish custom, appropriate for feast day of St. James the Greater

- Recalling gleaning instructions and, by extension, charity, appropriate for fundraiser

- Recalling Greek figures of autumn, appropriate for autumn equinox

- Recalling general association with joy, appropriate for adoption; Advent; birth; family/general birthday; Friendship Day; men's festivals; namegiving; ordination; peace celebration; remarriage; social debut; wedding; women's festivals

## Symbolic Uses of the Raisin

- Recalling literary connection with shattered dreams, appropriate for divorce; loss; separation

- Recalling funerary connection, appropriate for funeral; requiem; wake

- Recalling Abigail's mission of peace, appropriate for peace celebrations; reconciliation

## Symbolic Use of the Black Currant

- Recalling medicinal use for quinsy, appropriate for feast day of St. Blaise, invoked against throat ailments

# Grapefruit

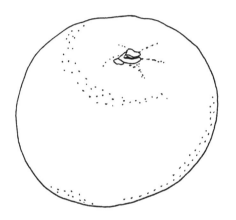

The grapefruit has one of the most complex family trees of any fruit. It is descended from the pomelo, itself a hybrid of the Oriental pummelo, which was brought to the West Indies in the 1700s. According to legend, the Scottish captain of the ship that brought the fruit to the Indies was named Shaddock (or Chaddock), and consequently grapefruits were sometimes called shaddocks. Its botanical name, *Citrus paradisi*, means "Garden (or park) **citron** tree." Appropriately, the fruit was once known as "Adam's **apple**." The fruit's common name refers to the fruit's **grape**-like clusterings on the tree.

Ethnic     In the Orient, grapefruits are a symbol of good health (see also **lemon, lime** [in **lemon**]). Because of their initial scarcity and high cost, they also represent luxury (see also **chestnut, quince**).

Europeans used grapefruits medicinally for over three hundred years.

Citrus seeds, in particular those of the grapefruit, are used today to make a male aphrodisiac in Japan.

Although the fruit is usually eaten for breakfast or as an appetizer in the west, in some middle-Eastern countries, it is a popular dessert.

Literary/Artistic     Grapefruits were once called "forbidden fruit" because of their bitter taste. They were also known as "Adam's **apples**" (see introductory remarks).

The fruit has no classical symbolism, but because of the famous breakfast scene in *Public Enemy* (1931), in which Jimmy Cagney pushes a grapefruit into Mae Clarke's face, the fruit represents romantic alienation—a symbolism reinforced by the bitter taste of the fruit.

## Symbolic Uses of the Grapefruit

- Recalling symbolism of romantic alienation, appropriate for divorce; separation

- Recalling Oriental symbolism of good health, appropriate for get well soon; recovery; also appropriate for feasts days of Sts. Luke, patron of physicians, and Camillus, patron of nurses and the sick, and saints invoked against illnesses

- Recalling alleged aphrodisiac properties, appropriate for St. Valentine's Day

# Lemon

## *with notes on Lime*

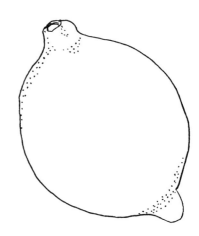

Probably of Asian origin, the lemon's botanical name, *Citrus limon*, may be translated "lemon-**citron** tree." Lemons were once known as **citrons**, and still are in France. Both lemons and **oranges** arrived in Europe via India about 1200 C.E. Their common name, like the **lime's**, has been derived from the Arabic *lim*, meaning, loosely, "**citron**-like fruit."

**Christian**  In early Christian art, lemons represented loyalty or allegiance to God. They were occasionally used as an emblem of Mary (see also **almond, apple, cherry, olive, raspberry, strawberry, walnut**). Lemons have been suggested as the fruit of the Tree of Knowledge, an apt choice in view of the lemon's noted bitterness (see also **apple, banana, fig, orange, pomegranate, quince, tomato**).

**Ethnic**  A nineteenth-century account relates that images of Christ were carried around Greek villages on Good Friday on biers decorated with lemons and flowers, accompanied by priests and the faithful. The biers were then taken into the church for more services, which culminated at the midnight hour before Easter Sunday, with jubilation among the congregation and fireworks set off in the village.

A lemon was sometimes substituted in the Italian ill-wishing charm described in the **orange** chapter (see also **lime**).

Lemons symbolize faithful love, and the Victorians used lemon blossoms as an emblem of fidelity.

**Literary/Artistic**  The nursery rhyme "**Oranges** and Lemons" is recalled in an annual children's service in the London church of St. Clement's Dane, at the close of which each child receives one each of the two fruits.

"To feel a right lemon" is to feel foolish or out of place (see also **banana**).

Useless items, especially cars, are dubbed lemons. (I recall a billboard lambasting one car manufacturer's products as such at an intersection in St. Louis some years ago; it was said to have been erected by a dissatisfied customer.)

"The answer's a lemon" is an appropriate reply to questions considered impertinent or intrusive. It has, however, been advised that should life hand one a metaphorical lemon, one should make lemonade. In this instance, the lemon stands for optimism and triumph over adversity.

The fruit's cleansing and astringent properties represent a fresh start or new beginning, and its zest makes it emblematic of enthusiasm.

Oliver Goldsmith mentions the fruit in *She Stoops to Conquer* (1773), when a character promises to appear in less time than it takes to squeeze a lemon.

"Squeezing until the pips squeak," meaning to extract everything possible from a person or situation, is usually connected with lemons, the fruit most likely to have its juice extracted for culinary use. A specific use of this phrase was made by Sir Eric Geddes in 1918, vis-à-vis German liability after the war. His statement, though shocking, was considered an accurate reflection of much British sentiment of the time.

## Medicinal

European herbalists once recommended pearls dissolved in lemon juice as a treatment for epilepsy; Ben Johnson refers to this cure in *The Alchemist* (1610).

Lemon juice, as well as that of the **lime**, was used as an anti-scurvy measure in the nineteenth century British navy, albeit less commonly than the latter. Both are therefore emblematic of good health (see also **grapefruit**).

Americans prescribed lemonade for the alleviation of measles, no doubt because of the fruit's well-known bleaching properties.

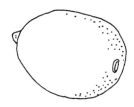

# Lime

The lime's botanical name, *Citrus aurantifolia*, means "orange-leafed **citron** tree." It probably originated in Asia. Its common name, like the **lemon's,** is derived from the Arabic *lim*, meaning, loosely, "**citron**-like fruit." In French, limes are *limons*.

Ethnic

Malayan miners reportedly regarded limes as forbidden food. It is said that members of theatrical companies in Malaysia regarded lime trees as their special guardians.

In India, they were thought to add particular potency to ill-wishing charms (see also **lemon, orange**).

The term "limey," used of a Briton, derives from the consumption of its juice and that of other citrus fruits, as an anti-scurvy measure aboard British ships. A mid-nineteenth-century manual advises captains to issue crews on salted meat rations a brew of **lemon** or lime juice, sugar and vinegar every ten days. Limes and **lemons** therefore represent both travel and good health (see also **grapefruit**). From the navy usage, "lime juicer" came to be applied to British ships and also, in Australia in the last century, to newly arrived immigrants.

## Symbolic Uses of the Lemon

- Recalling Victorian symbolism of fidelity, appropriate for remarriage; wedding

- Recalling symbolism of zest/enthusiasm, appropriate for dedication

- Recalling nursery rhyme, appropriate for children's birthdays; Children's Day; St. Clement's Day and, recalling his role as patron of sailors, appropriate for Armed Forces Day; enlistment; military discharge; also appropriate for feast day of St. Nicholas, patron of children

- Recalling lemon's sourness, appropriate for audit; divorce; separation; (on a humorous note) Over-the-Hill (40th) birthday; mother-in-law's birthday; Mother-in-Law's Day

- Recalling medicinal use and connection with good health, appropriate for get well soon; recovery; also appropriate for feast days of Sts. Luke, patron of physicians, and Camillus, patron of nurses and the sick, and saints invoked against illnesses

- Recalling Marian symbolism, appropriate for Marian festivals

- Recalling medicinal use, appropriate for feast day of St. Vitus, invoked against epilepsy and motor ailments

- Recalling lemon's connection with fresh beginnings/new starts, appropriate for artistic/professional/social debut; beginning kindergarten/college/school; commencement; first word; graduation; groundbreaking; housewarming; leaving home; new citizen; new home; new job; new venture; New Year's Day; New Year's Eve; premiere

- Recalling connection with travel, appropriate for bon voyage; first driver's license; first step; launching; leaving home

- Recalling Greek custom, appropriate for Good Friday

## Symbolic Uses of the Lime

- Recalling colloquialism for a Briton, appropriate for feast days of Sts. Andrew, David, George, and Patrick, patrons of Scotland, Wales, England, and Ireland, respectively

- Recalling medicinal use and connection with good health, appropriate for get well soon; recovery; also appropriate for feast days of Sts. Luke, patron of physicians, Camillus, patron of nurses and the sick, and saints invoked against illnesses

- Recalling Malaysian actors' belief, appropriate for premiere; school play

- Recalling colloquialism for a new immigrant, appropriate for Columbus Day; new citizen; new immigrant; also appropriate for feast day of St. Frances Cabrini, patron of immigrants

- Recalling connection with travel, appropriate for bon voyage; first driver's license; first step; launching; leaving home

# Melon

## with notes on Gourd

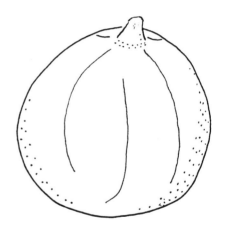

Like cucumbers, squash, and **pumpkins**, melons belong to the **gourd** family. They appear to have originated in the Near East. They belong, as noted, to the genus *Cucurbita*, ("gourd"), and their common name is derived from *melopepon* (Greek, "**apple** gourd").

## Ethnic

Judging by the evidence of their tomb-paintings, melons were particular favorites of the Egyptian nobility.

In some Arabic countries today, eating a melon is said to bring good fortune, the symbolism of abundance being attached to its many seeds. In Europe, an old colloquialism for a piece of financial good fortune was "a melon" (see also **gourd**).

Melons are a traditional New Year gift in Hong Kong and Singapore (see also **orange**). In China, during the New Year celebrations, it is customary to eat a steamed melon filled with chicken and vegetables and carved with a dragon in its skin, representing riches and good fortune.

Melons, cakes, **peaches**, and **pears** are offered by the Japanese during Tanabata-Matsuri ("Weaving-loom Festival," also known as the Star Festival) in July. The celebration recalls the story of Princess Shokujo, a beautiful and talented weaver who fell in love with the humble herdsman Kengyu. They were permitted to marry but subsequently neglected their duties and were punished by being placed at opposite ends of the Milky Way, meeting only once a year by crossing a bridge of magpies. The princess is represented by Vega and the herdsman by Altair, which supposedly meet on this night, when the Milky Way is said to be seen clearly for the first time in the year.

Islamic       Such is the reverence in which the Prophet is held that, according to a
              nineteenth-century work, one *imam* (Arabic, "leader," i.e., of prayers) refused to eat
              watermelons on the grounds that while the Prophet certainly ate them, it was not
              recorded how they were prepared (whether the rinds were left on or discarded before
              eating, and so on).*

Judaic        During their wanderings, the Children of Israel complain at having only manna to eat,
              remembering the melons, fish, and assorted vegetables they ate in Egypt (Numbers
              11:5). Thus melons, as well as the vegetables mentioned, may be used as an emblem of
              ingratitude.**

              Certain boulders on Mount Carmel on the Israeli coast are nicknamed "Elijah's melons,"
              from a folktale about a local landowner who refused Elijah hospitality, whereupon the
              former's melons were turned to stone (for similar stories about the Buddhist priest
              Kobo-Daishi, see also **chestnut, peach, pear**). (It was upon Mount Carmel that Elijah
              defeated several hundred priests of false gods by proving only the Lord could kindle
              flames under a sacrifice by divine intervention, as related in I Kings 18:19-39.)

---

*  Lane, *Manners and Customs of the Modern Egyptians*, 1836, quoted in Lippman,
   *Understanding Islam*, 1990.

** A curious echo of this appeared in an Associated Press obituary for Jiang Qing, imprisoned
   widow of Mao Tse-Tung. Although her daughter came to see her from time to time, she did not
   attempt to get her released. It was reported that on one occasion Jiang-Qing threw a watermelon
   to the ground, complaining of her child's heartlessness and lack of caring (*Chicago Tribune*
   [June 5, 1991]; Jiang Qing had died the month before).

## Literary/Artistic

According to an eyewitness account in the Logan County (Illinois) archives, at a meeting on the town site where lots were sold, Abraham Lincoln "christened" the town named after him (he had been involved in the legal work relating to its founding) by cutting a watermelon and allowing the juice to drip on the ground. This event (August 27, 1853) is commemorated by a statuette of a watermelon at the Lincoln Rail Depot.

Two watermelons that had (appropriately) been used for fishing-line buoys were an unusual exhibit in a nineteenth-century fisheries exhibition in Britain.

The watermelon's negative stereotypical role in the black experience was parodied in an exhibition held in Chicago in early 1991 by members of the Black Artist's Guild, entitled "The Return of the Watermelon: The Redefining of a Stereotype," in which the fruit played a pivotal role (usually an unexpected one).

It was, however, the Mexican painter, Rufino Tamayo, of whom it was said (according to an Associated Press obituary\*) that watermelons, because of their prominence in his work, had played the same role for him as **apples** had in the paintings of the French artist Paul Cezanne.

Like **strawberries**, melons have long been connected with summer (see also **apple, pear, pomegranate**). However, in *A Compendious Regyment or A Dietary of Helth*, the sixteenth-century writer Andrew Boorde made the startling assertion that melons produced "euyl humoures" in the eater, a claim at variance with the fruit's generally sunny reputation.

---

\*  *Chicago Tribune* (June 25, 1991).

Robert Browning describes the flower of the melon as "gaudy," though praises the humble British buttercup, in *Home Thoughts, from Abroad* (1845). Alfred, Lord Tennyson, characterizes the British gentleman as one who patronizes charities, writes pamphlets, and raises prizewinning livestock, pines, and large melons (*The Princess: A Medley* [1847]).

# *Gourd*

Native to both Old and New Worlds, the gourd gave its name to the genus *Cucurbita*, "gourd." Its common name is derived from the Middle English "gourde."

## Buddhist

In Japan, offerings made to the souls of the dead during O'Bon Matsuri (loosely, "Festival of the Departed"; also known as the Festival of Lanterns, from the many lit during it) include the favorite foods of the departed as well as gourds, eggplants, and potatoes.

## Christian

Pilgrims and other travelers commonly used gourds as water canteens. A major destination for pilgrimage in medieval times was Spain, where the reputed relics of St. James the Greater lay at Santiago de Compostela. He was shown in Christian art as a pilgrim, often carrying a gourd water bottle. Because of this connection with travel, gourds were also emblematic of Gabriel, messenger of God (see also **olive**) and Raphael, patron of travelers (see also **citron, hazel, walnut**); curiously, they were not depicted with St. Christopher (see also **citron, date, hazel, walnut**).

Because of the story of Jonah (see Judaic), the gourd represented protection in Christian art. If shown with an **apple,** which stands for temptation or evil, it could mean either protection from, or rejection of, one or both (see Judaic). A similar pairing of **apples** and cucumbers, a member of the gourd family, appears in Carlo Crivelli's *Madonna and Child* (c. 1480). In this painting, the cucumbers are taken to refer to Jonah's gourd and to symbolize resurrection, while the **apple** is emblematic of sin, from whose taint Mary is free (for other Marian symbolism, see also **almond, apple, cherry. lemon, olive, raspberry, strawberry, walnut**).

Ethnic

To Native American tribes of North Dakota, wild swans represented gourds, geese represented maize, and ducks represented beans; all three birds featured in spring corn medicine ceremonies honoring the Old Woman of the Crops.

Traditional wedding celebrations among the Swazi of southeast Africa include the bride dancing beside a sleeping mat, a headrest, and a calabash gourd containing beer, items symbolizing the new home to which she will go.

Houngans (voodoo priests) carried assons, calabash gourd rattles, as a sign of their authority and for use in rituals.

Initiation rites of the Gimi people of Papua New Guinea begin with a confrontation, when the boys are menaced by men in hideous gourd masks who threaten them harm if they reveal that the sound of certain jungle "birds" is, in fact, that of bamboo flutes, which women must never see.

Gourds are used as rain charms in many countries. In some rituals, pebbles are rattled in them to mimic thunder, and in others water is poured into, out of, or carried around in them as an emblem of rain.

In China, gourds were used to symbolize children (see also **pomegranate**) and could also represent magic and the unknown.

A Japanese proverb notes that it is fruitless to try to catch a wriggly fish by using a gourd, a warning to use the right tools for the job in hand.

It was once the custom in Provence, France, to stone a figure of Carnival on Ash Wednesday, after a parade in which celebrants drank wine from gourds (see also **chestnut**).

According to a Santal folktale from India, two sisters go to gather fruit. The elder goes to fetch water, and while she is away, her younger sister hides in a tree from a troop of monkeys. Unfortunately, one attacks and eats her. Meanwhile, the older sister has been seen by a passing rajah, who marries her. The monkey who ate the other sister dies, and a gourd springs from its body. A yogi takes one of its fruits and makes a musical instrument, which assumes the voice of the dead sister, telling of her fate. The older sister obtains it by trickery and keeps it hidden, but when no one is about, the younger sister emerges. Eventually the rajah sees her and takes her as another wife.

Gourds are used in many countries for making musical instruments such as the African bow-harp with calabash body; India's *vina*, which uses gourds as resonators; and the *ipu* or gourd drum of Hawaii. In Chinese music, one of the eight traditional categories is named after the gourd, and a prominent instrument in their classical orchestras is the *sheng*, a type of mouth-organ made from a small gourd fitted with fourteen or more pipes.

In Franco-American slang, a gourd was a dollar and *gourdes* are units of currency in present-day Haiti.*

**Judaic**  Jonah 4 relates that a gourd plant sprang up to shade Jonah as he sat outside Nineveh, waiting to see the city's destruction. It has been suggested that the gourd plant

---

* Soo Ethnic entry in **melon** for another monetary reference.

mentioned in the text was either a bottle gourd, a castor oil plant, or a cucumber. However, the gourd withers after a day, and Nineveh is spared on account of those of its inhabitants being unable to distinguish between left and right hands (meaning children) and its cattle (innocent beasts). The narrative emphasizes divine mercy, and the gourd thus represents this as well as reconciliation and the transience of life.

In II Kings 4:38-41, poisonous gourds are made into pottage, but Elisha instructs that meal be added, and the poison is thus counteracted (see Christian). These gourds may have been colocynths, a vine whose fruit is a purgative.

## Literary/Artistic

In Taoist art, a gourd from which mist rises represents the spirit ascending to heaven. Thus, it also symbolizes Li T'ien-kuai, who ascended there for seven days but was unable to reenter his body upon his return; thus he was forced to assume that of a beggar, another form in which he appears in art. The gourd's connection with immortality gives it the symbolism of longevity, although another interpretation suggests that this relates to the sprawling length of the gourd vine.

## *Symbolic Uses of the Melon (and/or Gourd, where noted)*

- Recalling Arabic connection with good fortune, appropriate for good fortune; promotion; reaching goal

- Recalling traditional New Year gift, appropriate for New Year's Day; New Year's Eve

- Recalling gourd's symbolism in Christian art, appropriate for feast day of St. James the Greater

- Recalling Nineveh's cattle, appropriate for feast day of St. Francis, patron of animals

- Recalling gourd's artistic symbolism of longevity, appropriate for adoption; birth; family/general birthday

- Recalling gourd's connection with the transience of life in Jonah, appropriate for anniversary of loss; birthday of departed; funeral; Memorial Day; remembering departed; requiem; wake

- Recalling gourd's use for musical instruments, appropriate for concert; recital; also appropriate for feast day of St. Cecilia, patron of musicians

- Recalling Judaic connection with ingratitude, appropriate for divorce; separation

- Recalling connection with summer, appropriate for Midsummer's Day; Midsummer's Eve; summer solstice

- Recalling Nineveh's children, appropriate for Children's Day; Holy Innocents Day

- Recalling gourd's Taoist symbolism, appropriate for Ascension Day

- Recalling gourd's connection with reconciliation in Jonah, appropriate for peace celebration; reconciliation

- Recalling gourd's connection with travel/pilgrimage, appropriate for welcome home; also appropriate for feast days of Sts. Christopher and Raphael, patrons of travelers; first driver's license; first step; pilgrimage

- Recalling gourd's rain-making role, appropriate for planting; Rogation Days, and, recalling tradition that rain on his feast day foretells forty more wet days, St. Swithin's Day

## Symbolic Uses of the Watermelon

- Recalling Islamic reverence for the Prophet, appropriate for dedication; ordination

- Recalling role in Lincoln lore, appropriate for baptism; namegiving; also appropriate for Lincoln's birthday

- Recalling connection with fishing, appropriate for feast days of Sts. Andrew and Peter, James and John

# *Olive*

Olives derive their name from the Latin *oliva*, meaning "olive" or "olive tree." Their botanical name, *Olea europaea*, means "European olive tree." Thought to have originated in the Syrian area, olives have long been one of the most important crops in the Near East and Mediterranean countries.

**Christian**    In Christian art, Gabriel is sometimes shown carrying the olive branch of peace, referring to that which will follow the Final Judgment (see also **gourd** [in **melon**]).

Olives are also occasionally used as an emblem of Mary (see also **almond, apple, cherry, lemon, raspberry, strawberry, walnut**).

Romans 11:16-24 mentions the olive tree of faith, comparing the righteous cleaving to God as grafts to the tree.

Matthew 25:1-13 relates the parable of the ten virgins: the five wise maidens having oil (made from olives) for their lamps and thus able to rejoice when the bridegroom arrives, whereas their five foolish colleagues, lightless because they have no oil, are not admitted to the celebrations. The message of this parable is that one should be vigilant, for no one knows when Christ will come (v. 13).

Jesus was betrayed in Gethsemane on the Mount of Olives. "Gethsemane" is Aramaic for "oil press," recalling both the **grape's** symbolism of sacrifice (because, like olives squeezed for oil, **grapes** must be destroyed to make wine) and the use of oil for anointing, "Messiah" being from the Hebrew *mashiach*, "anointed one" (see Judaic).

**Ethnic**    Serbians and other Slavonic people were formerly of the custom of using olive wood, rather than the more usual oak, for Yule logs.

Cypriots burnt olive leaves as an aid to domestic harmony; a lidded goblet used for this purpose can be seen in the immigration museum on Ellis Island.

A Catalan remedy for snakebite (see also **walnut**) was poultices of olive leaves, perhaps recalling the use of olive twigs to ritually expel evil from dwellings, thus, as it were, beginning afresh. Similarly, a Portuguese spell against evil spirits involves salt, incense, rye, nine drops of olive oil, and appropriate prayers.

Greek sailors sometimes toss olive branches on the sea as they set sail, in hopes of calm waters and a safe voyage.

Brides in ancient Greece wore olive-leaf chaplets as a symbol of fertility; olives also symbolized the harvest and autumn (see also **grape**; see Literary/Artistic).

Like the **fig** and **grape**, olives were sacred in Crete.

Olive branches are an Italian charm against evil.

**Islamic**    Al-Qur'an notes that olives, **dates**, and **grapes**, being, like everything, Allah's work, are things upon which believers should ponder (Surah XIII, *Ar-Ra'd* ["The Thunder"], v. 4; Surah XVI, *An-Nahl* ["The Bee"], vv. 11, 67).

Surah XXIII, *Al-Mu'minun* ("The Believers") v. 20, mentions a tree, evidently an olive, springing from Mount Sinai, and providing both oil and "relish." The symbolic aspect of this passage is noteworthy if it is interpreted as referring to the Commandments given to Moses on the mountain.

In Surah XXIV, *An-Nur* ("The Light"), the light of Allah in the Muslim home is compared to a lamp filled with blessed olive oil from a tree of neither east nor west.

The Prophet swore by both the olive and **fig** (Al-Qur'an, Surah XCV, *At-Tin* ["The Fig"], v. 1).

**Judaic**

The dove brought an olive leaf back to the Ark as a sign that the Flood had subsided (Genesis 8:11). Mediterranean folklore has it that the tree from which the leaf came was one which had grown out of Adam's grave.

Olive oil was used for lighting, including holy lamps (Exodus 27:20). It was also used for anointing kings and high priests (Exodus 28:41; I Samuel 10:1). The ritual cleansing of lepers included anointing the sufferer with oil and offering seven sprinkles of it to the Lord (Leviticus 14:15-18).

The olive is mentioned with **fig, grape**vine, and **pomegranate** as growing in the Promised Land (Deuteronomy 8:8).

Olive wood was used in the construction of the Temple in Jerusalem for doors (I Kings 6:31), door posts (I Kings 6:33), and decorative cherubs (I Kings 6:23).

Mingled flour and oil were among offerings to be made to the Lord (see, for example, Numbers 28:5).

Psalms 128:3 likens children to olive trees (see Literary/Artistic) and a wife to a **grape**vine.

Judges 9:8-15 relates a parable concerning an upstart claimant to the throne, in which the olive declines Kingship of the Trees on account of its "fatness" (see also **blackberry, fig, grape**).

Deuteronomy 24:19-21 instructs that olives and **grapes** be among crops whose gleanings are to be left at harvest-time for strangers, orphans, and widows.

Chapter 4 of Zechariah relates a vision of a golden candlestick flanked by olive trees (vv. 2-3) usually taken to mean Zerubbabel and Jeshua, governor and high priest respectively, who returned with other exiles from Babylon to rebuild the Temple (see Ezra 1:3). Zerubbabel was not only governor but also descended from King Jeconiah. The golden candlestick is considered emblematic of the Lord, or, alternatively, Israel.

Zechariah 14:4 states that when the Day of the Lord arrives, the Messiah will stand on the Mount of Olives (see Christian). It is for this reason that some Orthodox Jews wish to be interred on the Mount, for by tradition it is there that the resurrection of the dead will begin.

Jeremiah 11:16 describes a fruiting olive tree upon which fire is kindled (i.e., it is struck by lightning). Here the tree represents Israel, upon whom divine wrath will fall.

Hanukkah (Hebrew, "dedication") commemorates the 25th of Kislev, 165 B.C.E., when the Temple in Jerusalem was rededicated by Judas the Maccabee. This rededication followed a guerrilla war sparked by attempts to introduce Greek religious practices there and the resulting desecration of the Temple, as related in I and II Maccabees. It is said that a small amount of oil miraculously kept the sacred lamps burning for eight days, hence the celebration's other name, the Feast of Lights. The eight-day observance falls in December, and *latkes* (potato pancakes, a fried food recalling the oil) are traditionally served during it.

In contemporary Israel, olives are eaten during Tu Bi-Shevat (Hebrew, "15th of Shevat," a month corresponding to late January/early February). Also known as the New Year for Trees, its origin are connected with fruit tithes anciently due at this time. Various customs grew up around the date, including eating fruits which grew in Israel. Ashkenazic Jews commonly ate fifteen kinds, after the date of the festival. The character of Tu Bi- Shevat is now more secular, but it is customary to mark it by planting trees and eating of the Seven Species of Israel, namely, barley, **figs**, honey (see date), **grapes**, olives, **pomegranates**, and wheat, all of which grow in the Promised Land (Deuteronomy 8:8) (see also **almond**).

Two folk remedies among many in the Talmud are said to cure toothaches (roasted olive stones applied to the tooth [see also **apricot, fig, walnut**]) and hangovers (rubbing salt and olive oil into the soles and palms, with appropriate prayers).

## Literary/Artistic

Above all, an olive branch symbolizes peace. "Offering an olive branch" means making overtures for it, and "pouring (olive) oil on troubled waters" means calming fury. In European art, figures of Peace not only carried olive branches but were often crowned with olive-leaf chaplets. Appropriately, the Romans declared that it took a lengthy period of peace (five years) to allow olives and **grapes** to come to full fruition, and good crops and vintages to be produced.

Greek statues of autumn carried olive boughs and **grape**vines. In sixteenth-century Spanish literature, the legendary hero Palmerin de Oliva took his name from the grove of **date** palms and olive trees in which his mother—supposedly of royal blood—abandoned him. The pairing of species is interesting in view of the story of Leto (see Mythological; see also **cherry, plum**).

"Olive branches," as a jocular term for children (derived from Psalm 128; see Judaic), appears in Jane Austen's *Pride and Prejudice* (1813) and Charles Dickens' *Nicholas Nickleby* (1838-39).

## Mythological

In Greek mythology, Poseidon, god of the sea, claimed land on the Acropolis in Athens. Athene, goddess of wisdom, disputed this, causing the first olive tree to grow on the spot. Poseidon therefore created a salt water well nearby, but the council of gods ruled that, as Athene had given humankind the greater gift, the land was hers. It is recorded that as late as 2 C.E. visitors were being shown her olive tree (see also **fig**).

When Prometheus stole fire from the gods for humankind, Zeus ordered him chained and punished. Hercules, however, rescued Prometheus and, according to legend, donned an olive leaf chaplet (emblematic of the chains) as a token of his victory. Winners of women's footraces honoring Hera, wife of Zeus, were awarded similar chaplets (perhaps with ironic intent) as were Olympic athletes, whose games honored Zeus. The winner of the chariot race at Athenian games received the magnificent prize of one hundred vases of olive oil.

In Roman mythology, the corn goddess Ceres (Greek Demeter), during her search for her lost daughter, Proserpine (see also **pomegranate**), lived for a time under an olive tree (see also **fig**). Some versions of the story of the birth of Apollo and Artemis mention that their mother Leto was supported by an olive tree and **date** palm during delivery (see also **cherry, plum**). The same two trees appear in a birth story from Spanish literature (see Literary/Artistic).

## *Symbolic Uses of the Olive*

- Recalling connection with autumn, appropriate for autumn equinox

- Recalling Marian symbolism, appropriate for Marian festivals

- Recalling symbolism in Christian art, appropriate for feast day of Gabriel

- Recalling toothache remedy mentioned in the Talmud, appropriate for first tooth; also appropriate for feast day of St. Apollonia, invoked against toothaches

- Recalling connection with peace, appropriate for negotiation; peace celebration; reconciliation

- Recalling use to sweep out evil/begin afresh, appropriate for commencement; artistic/professional/social debut; graduation; new job; new venture; New Year's Day; New Year's Eve; premiere; remarriage

- Recalling Greek symbolism of the harvest, appropriate for harvest festival; Kwanzaa; Thanksgiving

- Recalling use for anointing, appropriate for baptism; dedication; namegiving; ordination

- Recalling gleaning instructions and, by extension, charity, appropriate for fundraiser

- Recalling Greek sailors' charm for a safe voyage, appropriate for bon voyage; first driver's license; launching; leaving home

- Recalling role in Tu Bi-Shevat, appropriate for Arbor Day

# Orange

## with notes on Tangerine

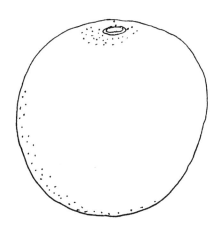

The orange is believed to be a native of India, although its botanical name, *Citrus sinensis* ("**citron** tree [of] China"), reflects the old belief that it originated in that country. Its common name derives from the Sanskrit *naranga*, meaning, loosely, "sweet- scented." Like **lemons**, oranges arrived in Europe via India about 1200 B.C.E.

**Christian**  Oranges have been suggested as the fruit of the Tree of Knowledge (see also **apple, banana, fig, lemon, pomegranate, quince, tomato**). For this reason, in Christian art, oranges symbolize the Garden of Eden, wisdom, and glory.

Three oranges (interpreted by some as golden **apples**) represent St. Nicholas. They symbolize either bags of gold which he left for three dowerless girls, or the heads of three murdered children, which, according to medieval legend, he restored to life.

A nineteenth-century writer records the tradition that St. Dominic planted an orange tree in the garden of St. Sabina's Convent in Rome.

**Ethnic**  In the Orient, oranges were regarded as sacred, a heavenly fruit representing everlasting life. A Chinese legend tells of temple-grown oranges, which granted children to infertile women (see also **coconut, fig, pomegranate**).

In many parts of Italy, oranges are traditional fare for St. Joseph's Day.

In Japan, traditional decorations for the New Year include an orange, the spoken Japanese for which resembles the Chinese for, loosely, "from one generation to the next" (see **plum** for complete list).

The fruit's shape and glowing color readily suggest coins and thus prosperity, generosity, and good fortune. An even number of oranges is a traditional New Year gift in China and Singapore, a custom giving them the secondary symbolism of a new beginning (see also **melon**).

An orange or **tangerine** is one of three traditional toe-stuffers for Christmas stockings, the others being an **apple** and nuts. In parts of southern Mexico, orange leaves scent the water with which women who have recently borne a child are bathed (see also **banana, coconut, date**).

The first oranges in America were reportedly grown near St. Augustine in Florida.

Seminole Indians reputedly enjoyed honey-soaked oranges, whilst medieval English aristocrats considered fried oranges a particular delicacy—as succinct a summing-up of international culinary differences as can be found.

The oranges and **lemons** mentioned in the nursery rhyme of the same name are remembered in a distribution of the two citruses after children's services held annually at the Church of St. Clement's Dane, London. Cheesecake decorated with fresh or candied orange slices is known as St. Clement's Cheesecake.

Orange blossoms have strong connections with purity; in Japan, they represent chaste affection, and Syrian brides wore chaplets of orange flowers symbolizing virginity. Its use for weddings arrived in England via the continent about the mid-nineteenth century. The custom gave rise to the saying "to hunt orange blossom," used of a man seeking a wife (see also **peach**).

## Literary/Artistic

In Christian art, the Christ Child is often depicted holding an orange, a symbol of glory.

"Comparing **apples** to oranges" is useless, there being no common ground.

## Medicinal

Oranges were considered effective antidotes to poison. In European wicca,* they represented the heart and thus figured in both death and love charms. Although a citrus

---

\* Wicca isa pre-Christian religion, which is now generally, though erroneously, known as witchcraft.

fruit, the orange does not seem to have acquired the symbolism of good health connected with the **grapefruit, lemon**, or **lime** (see **lemon**). An Italian ill-wishing charm involved pinning the name of a person to an orange; the victim would sicken as the fruit rotted away. A **lemon** was sometimes substituted in this charm (see also **lime** [in **lemon**]).

## Mythological

Orange blossoms were sacred to the virginal Roman lunar goddess Diana (Greek Artemis) (see also **apple, pear**). This may have founded the superstition that bridal orange blossoms must be disposed of immediately after the wedding for fear the marriage would be childless.

The golden **apples** of various myths have been interpreted as oranges.

The fruit is also a symbol of the sun, and the orange sometimes substituted for the **apple** in the Yule boar's mouth has been viewed as representing the sun at the mid-winter solstice (see **tangerine**).

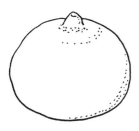

# *Tangerine*

Tangerines derive their name from the fact that they were once imported into Europe via Tangier, Morocco. They are also known as "Mandarin oranges" from their probable Chinese origin. The tangerine's botanical name, *Citrus reticulata*, means "netted **citron** tree," "netted" apparently referring to the fruit's markedly loose skin, which makes it particularly easy to peel away.

**Ethnic**

In Hong Kong, tangerines are considered fruits of good omen, and small potted tangerine trees are much favored for New Year decorations.

Tangerines sometimes substitute for the **orange** as a toe-stuffer in Christmas stockings (with **apple** and nuts).

Like the **orange**, the tangerine is a sun symbol.

## *Symbolic Uses of the Orange (and/or Tangerine, where noted)*

- Recalling nursery rhyme, appropriate for children's birthdays; Children's Day; St. Clement's Day and, recalling his role as patron of sailors, also appropriate for Armed Forces Day; enlistment; launching; military discharge

- Recalling symbolism in Christian art, appropriate for St. Nicholas' Day

- Recalling Italian custom, appropriate for St. Joseph's Day

- Recalling Oriental connection with generosity/good fortune, appropriate for baby shower; family/general birthday; bridal shower; Friendship Day; fundraiser; good fortune; retirement

- Recalling Christian symbolism of glory, appropriate for baptism; Christmas; college/high school reunion; confirmation; congratulations; artistic/professional/ social debut; Easter Sunday; Epiphany; first eucharist; long-service award; milestones; namegiving; Palm Sunday; premiere; promotion; reaching goal; recognition award; sports victory; wedding anniversary, especially 50th (golden)

- Recalling connection with moon-goddess, appropriate for full moon; lunar eclipse; new/quarter moon

- Recalling orange/tangerine's Oriental connection with new year/new beginning, appropriate for groundbreaking; housewarming; new citizen; new home; new immigrant; new job; new venture; New Year's Day; New Year's Eve; reconciliation; remarriage

- Recalling role in love charms, appropriate for St. Valentine's Day

- Recalling connection with purity, appropriate for wedding

- Recalling Christian symbolism of wisdom, appropriate for beginning kindergarten/college/school; commencement; graduation; reaching adulthood

- Recalling orange/tangerine's use as a symbol of the sun, appropriate for Groundhog Day; harvest festival; Kwanzaa; Midsummer's Day; Midsummer's Eve; planting; Rogation Days; solar eclipse; summer solstice; Thanksgiving; winter solstice

# *Peach*

Although the peach is thought to be of Chinese origin, it was once known as the "Persian **plum**" or "Persian **apple**." The fruit's botanical name reflects this tradition, being *Prunus persica*, "**plum** (of) Persia." From this, peaches were once called *persics* (still used in modern French), but their common name is derived from the fruit's name in Middle English, "peche."

**Buddhist**  The peach and **pear** are mentioned among fruits and vegetables turned to stone or otherwise rendered inedible in stories about the hospitality (or lack of it) encountered by the priest Kobo-Daishi (loosely translated, "great teacher who spreads laws"), founder of the Shingon branch of Buddhism\* (see also **chestnut**).

**Ethnic**  In the Orient, peach blossoms represent feminine beauty (see also **almond, cherry, plum**), and, in Taoist symbolism, virginity. In China, because of its connection with longevity (see Mythological), congratulations to new parents often have a peach motif. The fruit is also considered effective against evil, so carvings of peach-bearing branches were placed over doors to protect dwellings. Children still sometimes wear peach-stone amulets as a protective measure.

Branches of peach blossoms are the traditional decoration for the Japanese girls' festival held in March, Hina-Matsuri ("Doll Festival"), which is also known as the Peach Festival. During Hina-Matsuri, dolls dressed in Imperial court finery are displayed upon red-covered shelves, with miniature utensils and furniture. A strict etiquette is followed in their viewing. In Japan, peach flowers represent the feminine virtues of peace and gentleness, and the day of the festival is popular for weddings (the blossoms also symbolizes marital happiness).

In the Japanese floral calendar, March is represented by peach and **pear** blossoms (see also **cherry, plum**). Peaches are offered during their July Tanabata-Matsuri ("Weaving-loom Festival") (see also **melon, pear**).

---

\* For a similar story about Elijah, see **melon**.

European folklore states that when peach blossoms fall before spring is over, livestock will sicken.

The Victorian flower language endowed peach blossom with the message that the recipient had captured the giver's affection (see also **currant** [in **grape**]).

The peach and ice cream dessert "Peach Melba" was named after Dame Nellie Melba, the Australian opera singer. "Irish peaches," however, refer to the potato, that island's culinary mainstay, while the Cornish aptly describe the peach as a "suede **apple**."

## Literary/Artistic

A Japanese folktale tells of Momotaro ("peach Taro," the latter being a boy's name), commonly called "Little Peachling." According to the story, a woodcutter's wife finds a peach in a stream, and the boy emerges from the fruit. He lives with the couple and, when grown, wins an ogre's treasure with the aid of a dog, a monkey, and a pheasant, so that he and his foster parents can live happily ever after. His likeness is a popular decoration for the May Boy's Day Festival.

In underworld slang, "to peach" was to inform against someone, hence "peacher," an informant.

Colloquially, the loss of innocence is described as "the bloom (is) off the peach," a term sometimes also used of old looks.

In American slang, "peachy" is used to describe something good.

The **tomato's** botanical name means "edible wolf peach"; both fruits were once considered deadly.

According to a sixteenth-century herbal, peaches flower with **almonds**, thus making it one of the earliest to bloom, and emblematic of spring (see also **cherry, chestnut, pomegranate**).

## Medicinal

A sixteenth-century writer noted that peaches would "mollyfy the belly," and peach tea is a Native American measure for abating fever.

## Mythological

In Greco-Roman mythology, Hymen, god of marriage, was described as a beautiful young man, veiled, carrying a torch, and crowned with a chaplet of peach blossoms (see also **orange**).

According to Japanese mythology, Izanagi was pursued over the Reed Plains to a pass leading to the Dark Lands. Here he found a peach tree and used three of its fruits to route his attackers. He then declared that henceforth the fruit must render similar assistance to those in need of it. He and his wife Izanami were the first married couple and represented heavenly wisdom and truth (see also **plum**). Part of their story parallels those of Persephone and Proserpine (see also **pomegranate**), in that when Izanami dies, Izanagi follows her to the land of the dead. However, having eaten of its food, she cannot return to the living world, and Izanagi, appalled at her inevitable decay, flees (see also **apple**).

Peaches and **plums** grow on Mount Horai in the Japanese Paradise (see also **apple, cherry**).

According to Chinese legend, the peach goddess Hsi Wang Mu tends her trees in a garden to the west; each peach grants thirty centuries of life to the eater. The god of longevity, Shou Hsing, was originally mortal, but stole three peaches from the goddess;

he appears in Chinese art holding them, or emerging from one. Thus the Chinese said that eating peaches preserved the body from corruption, and the fruit therefore symbolized youth and immortality.

The persea, a fruit whose type is debated but which is usually equated with the peach, played a prominent role in Egyptian religion, because during coronation ceremonies, the pharaoh's throne name was written on the leaves of a persea at Ra's temple in Heliopolis (Greek, "sun city").* This was believed to bring the ruler a prosperous reign. Because peach leaves resemble the tongue, the tree was considered sacred to Harpocrates, the Egyptian god usually shown with his fingers across his lips, and thus regarded as the god of silence.** Similarly, truth was symbolized by a peach with one leaf on its stem.

---

* Known also as On (Egyptian, "sun," "light"), Heliopolis is by tradition the city in which Joseph, Mary, and Jesus lived in Egypt. The apt symbolism of the names of the city is noteworthy (see also **fig**).

** This gesture recalls Job signifying silence by laying his hand over his mouth (Job 40:4).

## Symbolic Uses of the Peach

- Recalling Victorian symbolism of captivation, appropriate for engagement; remarriage; wedding
- Recalling Egyptian connection with prosperity, appropriate for new venture; reaching goal
- Recalling Egyptian symbolism of truth, appropriate for jury duty
- Recalling colloquialism for potato, appropriate for feast day of St. Patrick, patron of Ireland
- Recalling decorative use for Hina-Matsuri, appropriate for girl's birthday; women's festivals
- Recalling connection with sun god, appropriate for solar eclipse; summer solstice
- Recalling derivation of Peach Melba, appropriate for concert; recital; also appropriate for feast day of St. Cecilia, patron of musicians

- Recalling colloquial connection with innocence, appropriate for Sweet Sixteen
- Recalling use as an emblem of spring, appropriate for spring equinox
- Recalling connection with Boy's Festival, appropriate for boy's birthday
- Recalling connection with Paradise, appropriate for funeral; wake
- Recalling connection with longevity, appropriate for adoption; birth; family/general birthday; retirement
- Recalling Chinese door decoration, appropriate for groundbreaking; new home; housewarming

# *Pear*

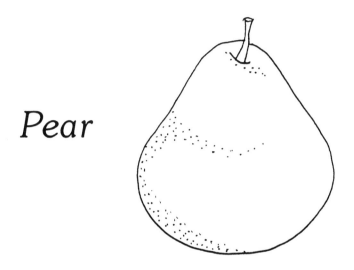

Pears have been cultivated from ancient times, having been known in the the Orient four thousand years ago and appearing in Egyptian funerary art. The fruit's common name is derived from the Latin *pirum*, "pear," which is echoed in its botanical name, *Pyrus communis*, meaning "common pear," via the Middle English "pere." The same Latin root provided the archaic "perry" for a pear tree, often used when referring to the wild variety, as well as the drink (see Ethnic). Pears probably originated in Asia.

**Buddhist**  When the priest Kobo-Daishi, founder of the Shingon branch of Buddhism, was wandering about in the guise of a beggar, he was treated well in some villages. In others, however, he was not, whereupon he caused wells to dry up and various fruits, notably pears and **peaches**, to turn into stone or otherwise be rendered inedible (see also **chestnut**).*

**Christian**  In Christian art, pears represent hope, divine love, and God's justice (see also **chestnut**; see Ethnic), a meaning evoked in Carlo Crivelli's *Madonna and Child* (c. 1490), in which the Child, gazing heavenward, holds a pear.

The fruit is one of four mentioned in a children's begging-song sung door-to-door on All Souls Day (see also **apple, cherry, plum**).

**Ethnic**  In parts of southern Belgium, it was formerly the custom on the first two Sundays of Lent to visit orchards and wave flaming torches under the branches of pear, **apple**, and **cherry** trees, with pleas for them to bear heavy crops of fruit.

Pear trees featured in a cattle-protection ceremony practiced by the Circassians of southern Russia. Every autumn, households cut down a pear tree and took it indoors, decorating it with candles and topping it with a cheese (perhaps an inducement to the cows to provide much milk). There was much celebration and merriment, but when the festivities ended, the tree was left outside with no further attention to it. This rather cavalier attitude is reminiscent of the old saying that something of little value is "not worth a pear" (see also **cherry, fig, gooseberry, persimmon**).

---

*  For a similar story about Elijah, see **melon**.

Pears and **apples** decorated a small tree carried by Summer in a seasonal mock battle with muffled-up Winter, which was held in some Bavarian villages on the fourth Sunday of Lent. In the sixteenth century, dried pears were permitted Lenten food and were given with milk and peas to mid-Lent visitors, who carried an effigy of Death door-to-door in Frankish villages in Germany, announcing that Death would soon be vanquished by the risen Lord.

In one Swiss canton, it was a pleasant custom to plant a pear tree to mark the birth of a girl (see also **apple, coconut**).

In the Japanese floral calendar, March is represented by pear and **peach** blossoms (see also **cherry, plum**). Offerings of pears, cakes, **melons**, and **peaches** are made during the Japanese Tanabata-Matsuri ("Weaving-loom Festival") in July.

According to Chinese legend, the wise Lord Shao held court under a pear tree, sitting in legal judgment. The pear therefore represents justice (see Christian; see also **chestnut**) and, by extension, good government.

Perry, the pear equivalent of **apple** cider (which in the UK is a highly intoxicating drink), was once known as "merry legs," from its effect.

Europeans know the familiar Bartlett pear as the *Bon Chrétien* (French, "Good Christian"), a tribute to its virtues. The same variety was also known as the Eusebian Pear, after the fourth-century bishop.

In the Victorian flower language, pear blossoms represented comfort; the fruit itself, affection.

Because an Imperial college of music was built in a pear orchard, Chinese musical actors were formerly known as the "Brethren of the Pear Orchard."

| Literary/Artistic | According to the nursery rhyme "I Had A Little Nutmeg," no less a person than the King of Spain's daughter came to see a magical tree which bore nothing but golden pears and silver nutmegs. |

Another name for hawthorn-berries is "pixie pears," the tree being considered sacred to the fairy folk (see also **blackberry, elderberry**).

The longevity of the pear is recalled in the folk-saying that, "Whoever plants an **apple** may well see its end, Whoever plants a pear, plants it for his friends," a sentiment expressed more succinctly, if pessimistically, in the variant, "Plant a pear / You plant it for your heirs."

The nineteenth-century colloquialism "as pert as a pearmonger" recalled the proverbial sauciness (sassiness) of itinerant fruit sellers.

In Benjamin Disraeli's *Sybil* (1845), a situation in which daring action is needed is characterized by the observation that the pear would be ripe for picking, was there only courage to do so.

The traditional Christmas carol "The Twelve Days of Christmas," which mentions a gift of a partridge roosting in a pear tree, is thought to be of French origin. It was an old Yuletide custom to walk around a pear tree three times; this was said to bring a vision of one's beloved. A more explicit interpretation notes that the pear was a phallic symbol in the Middle Ages, and the partridge a notorious emblem of lust.

The botanical name of the **persimmon** may be translated "God-Pear (of) Virginia."

**Medicinal**

The fruit was particularly popular during medieval times, and a pear preserve, *chardewardon* (French, "flesh of the Wardon," a type of pear then widely grown) was recommended for ailments of the stomach.

**Mythological**

In Greek mythology, pear trees were sacred to Hera, queen of the gods, and her statues were often made of its wood.

The pear's white blossom made it sacred to the moon and to lunar and virginal goddesses such as Artemis (Roman Diana; see also **apple, orange**), Athene, and the Roman goddess Luna. The tree's lunar aspect also connected it to the Greek goddess Hecate, a three-fold deity with particular importance in wicca* and the underworld, and Selene, the moon goddess honored by devotees at the beginning and middle of each moon cycle.

An Australian Aboriginal legend relates that Kaluru, the rain god, sent various animals and birds to observe a tribe which had grossly tormented one of their fellow creatures (an owl). For various reasons, all but the lizard fail in their task, although the honey-eater's excuse was that it had consumed wild pears and could not even recall seeing the miscreants. Judgment is passed on the tribe, and all perish in a flood sent by Kaluru, save for two children who are carried to higher ground by a wallaby and are subsequently raised by another tribe.

Pear wood gives a pleasant aroma when burnt and was much used for sacred fires, in particular the kindling for "need fires," for such important rituals as animal protection

---

* Wicca is a pre-Christian religion, which is now generally, though erroneously, known as witchcraft.

and crop magic. Its popularity for this purpose was especially widespread in the Balkans and eastern European countries (see also **fig, hazel**).

## Symbolic Uses of the Pear

- Recalling "Brethren of the Pear," appropriate for concert; recital; also appropriate for feast day of St. Cecilia, patron of musicians

- Recalling Victorian symbolism of comfort, appropriate for anniversary of loss; loss

- Recalling Chinese legend's connection with justice and, by extension, good government, appropriate for Election Day; taking office

- Recalling colloquial connection with sassiness, appropriate for children's birthdays (particularly teens')

- Recalling begging song, appropriate for All Souls Day

- Recalling Swiss custom, plant a pear tree to mark the adoption, birth, or birthday of a girl

- Recalling Christian symbolism of hope, appropriate for first wedding anniversary; get well soon; groundbreaking; housewarming; leaving home; negotiation; new home; new job; new venture; recovery; remarriage; wedding

- Recalling Victorian symbolism of affection, appropriate for adoption; birth; family/general birthday (particularly appropriate for twins' birthday); Friendship Day; Sweetest Day

- Recalling Christian symbolism of justice, appropriate for audit; peace celebration; reconciliation; also appropriate for feast day of St. Yves, patron of lawyers; jury duty

- Recalling Christian symbolism of divine love, appropriate for Christmas; Easter Sunday; Pentecost

- Recalling Bavarian connection with summer, appropriate for Midsummer's Day; Midsummer's Eve; summer solstice

- Recalling Disraeli's analogy for daring action, appropriate for sports victories

- Recalling Frankish custom, appropriate for Lent

- Recalling lunar connections, appropriate for full moon; lunar eclipse; new/quarter moon

- Recalling old name for Bartlett pear, appropriate for feast day of St. Eusebius of Vercelli

# Persimmon

Persimmons are mentioned in Captain John Smith's 1624 history of Virginia; he notes that the fruit was dried to make "pruines." The fruit's common name is of Algonquian origin, related to the Cree *pasiminan*, meaning "dried fruit." Their botanical name, *Diospyros virginiana*, can be translated as either "divine wheat (of) Virginia" or "God-**pear** (of) Virginia," apparently referring to the fruit's taste. Persimmons are native to America.

**Ethnic** American folklore claims that cutting persimmon seeds in half predicts winter weather, so that, for example, spoon- or shovel-shaped seeds foretell a hard winter with much snow.

Persimmon beer enjoyed a vogue in nineteenth-century America.

Persimmons were once known as "Virginian **date plums**" or "Indian **dates**."

In the Victorian flower language, persimmon blossoms conveyed a wish to be buried in the countryside.

**Literary/Artistic** Persimmons are mentioned in a number of colloquialisms. "Raking in the persimmons" means to be engaged in a profitable venture.

"The longest pole gets the persimmons" states the debatable point that the person with the most advantages gets success.

It was said to be useless to "take more than one bite at a persimmon," meaning something was of little or no value (see also **cherry, fig, gooseberry, pear**).

A Japanese screen by Sakai Hoitsu in the Metropolitan Museum of Art is decorated with a leafless, though fruiting, persimmon tree, representing autumn.

**Medicinal** Native Americans use preparations from the fruit for ailments as diverse as heartburn, liver problems, and sore throats.

Persimmons were used to treat fever in the American south.

## Symbolic Uses of the Persimmon

- Recalling Japanese symbolism of autumn, appropriate for autumn equinox

- Recalling medicinal use, appropriate for feast days of Sts. Blaise, invoked against throat ailments, and Domitian, invoked against fever

- Recalling connection with winter weather, appropriate for winter solstice

- Recalling colloquialism for profitable venture, appropriate for new job; new venture

- Recalling funerary connections, appropriate for birthday of departed; funeral; remembering departed; requiem; wake

- Recalling colloquialism connecting persimmons with success, appropriate for good fortune; reaching goal

# *Pineapple*

Pineapples seem to have originated in tropical South America. Known to the Incas, their Peruvian name was *ananas* (loosely, "fruit of excellence"). Their common name refers to their resemblance to a pinecone (with which they are interchangeable in heraldic art). Their botanical name, *Ananas comosus*, may be translated "leafy (or tufted) pineapple." The fruit is still known as an *ananas* in modern French.

**Ethnic**

In a Caribbean rite of manhood, barefoot youths ran through pineapple plantings, being expected to bear the resulting wounds without protest. Paradoxically, pineapple crowns were a symbol of hospitality in the same area.

A similar tradition appears in New England, where newly returned sea captains (whose cargoes often included exotic fruits) erected a pineapple on a post at their door as an indication both of a safe homecoming and that visitors were welcome. For this reason, pineapples remain a popular motif for door furniture and holiday decorations in coastal areas of New England. Similarly, representations of the fruit decorated plantation gates in the south.

**Literary/Artistic**

Because of their pleasing shape, pineapples were much used in architecture for finials and decorative details, especially in the Baroque period.

The fruit attracted many admirers in Europe, among them Sir Walter Raleigh, who termed it "the princess of fruits." One nineteenth-century writer called it the most delicious of all American fruits. The plant's crown of leaves gave it a royal air, which a sixteenth-century admirer declared to be the handiwork of the King of Kings. By the eighteenth century, pineapples were being sold for a king's ransom, Hugh Walpole recording in a letter written in 1746 that he had paid a guinea* for two of them. Richard Brinsley Sheridan describes a character in *The Rivals* (1775) as a "pineapple of politeness."

---

\* One pound one shilling in the old British sterling currency; one pound five pence in the current decimal coinage.

The many "eyes" of a pineapple are emblematic of vigilance. In 1940s underworld slang, a pineapple was a bomb, a term still used in military circles of a hand-grenade (see also **pomegranate**).

There is an amusing, though doubtless apocryphal, story about Louis XIV of France, that most hasty of monarchs.\* Having ordered the fruit specially grown, when presented with the first, he bit into it forthwith, garnering a mouthful of prickles for his pains and, so it is said, banishing pineapples from France forever. Pineapples are thus an excellent symbol of hastiness or impatience, although to the Victorians they represented perfection (see also **strawberry**).

## Mythological

It is said that a pineapple-topped pillar represented Marduk, the great Babylonian hero-god, and a pineapple was a symbol of Cybele, whose cult originated in Asia Minor (see also **almond, pomegranate**). However, in view of the fruit's late arrival in Europe, doubts have been cast upon these assertions, and it may be that these symbols were, in fact, pinecones (see introductory notes).

---

\* It was he who reportedly complained on one occasion that he had *almost* had to wait.

## Symbolic Uses of the Pineapple

- Recalling Caribbean symbol of hospitality, appropriate for housewarming; new home

- Recalling Caribbean manhood rites, appropriate for reaching adulthood

- Recalling fruit's New World origins, appropriate for Columbus Day

- Recalling New England connection with safe homecoming, appropriate for family reunion; homecoming (college); welcome home

- Recalling the fruit's many "eyes," appropriate for feast day of St. Lucy, invoked against eye ailments

- Recalling military slang, appropriate for Armed Forces Day; enlistment

- Recalling Louis XIV's hastiness, appropriate for separation

- Recalling connection with royalty, appropriate for family/general birthday; father's birthday; Father's Day; father-in-law's birthday; grandfather's birthday; grandmother's birthday; Grandparent's Day; mother's birthday; Mother's Day; mother-in-law's birthday; remarriage; wedding; wedding anniversary; welcome new baby

# *Plum*

## *with notes on Prune*

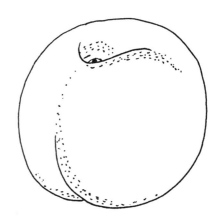

The plum is thought to have originated in western Asia. It belongs to the genus *Prunus*, which also includes the **almond, apricot, cherry**, and **peach**. Its botanical name, *Prunus domestica*, means "domestic plum." The plum's common name is derived from the High German *pflümo*, "plum" or "plum tree."

Christian    Plums are one of four fruits mentioned in a children's begging-song sung door-to-door on All Souls Day, the others being **apple, cherry**, and **pear**.

Ethnic    The Welsh say that when a plum tree blooms out of season, a family death is imminent.

According to Australian Aboriginal folklore, when the wild plum blossoms, the rainy season is at hand (see also **fig**); in the Orient, the spring rains are known as the "Plum Rains."

To the Chinese, the fruit represents strength and fidelity, and the flowers are emblems of feminine beauty and virtuous character (see also **almond, cherry, peach**). A bent branch of plum blossoms symbolizes vigor and sprightliness in old age.

Plum blossoms have more than one meaning to the Japanese. It is one of the traditional decorations for the New Year because it is first to bloom and so represents vigor.* Plum blossoms are also one of a number of traditional decorations for the backs of the bats used in New Year games of shuttlecock.

Pine, bamboo, and plum are often grouped together, and when so found are usually called "Winter Friends" (in China, plums symbolize winter). Branches of the three are placed in a vase on a bench beneath a painting of Izanami and Izanagi, the first married

---

* Other decorations include ferns, representing expanding good fortune, from the shape of their fronds; bamboo for fidelity; pine, meaning long life; an **orange**, representing "from one generation to the next," the spoken Japanese word for the fruit resembling a similar Chinese phrase with this meaning; and a lobster, its bent back representing age but expressing a hope for a young spirit.

couple (see **peach**), for traditional Japanese weddings. In this context, they represent long life, fidelity, and the wish for a happy and successful life together.

Plum blossoms, again representing vigor and good health, are one of the motifs on bags of sweetmeats given to Japanese children when they visit shrines during the November festival of Shichi-go-san ("7, 5, 3," the ages of participating children by Japanese reckoning; some would be a year younger because of the custom of counting children to be a year old at the beginning of the year following their birthdate, regardless of what month or day they were born).

Because the plum blooms early, another symbolism of the fruit is triumph.

According to an Oriental legend, the first plum tree sprang from the blood of a dragon (see also **grape**).

In the Japanese floral calendar, plum blossoms represent February (see also **cherry, peach, pear**).

## Literary/Artistic

Plums are mentioned in more than one nursery rhyme. The best-known is probably that relating the fight between the Lion and the Unicorn, during which some townfolk offer the brawling beasts bread (both brown and white loaves), while others offer plum-cake. Eventually, the dueling duo are drummed out of town. Another rhyme tells of two robins who go to town to buy some buns, but, unable to agree as to whether to purchase plain or plum, return home without either, a story pointing to the desirability of compromise. A third tells of a cat trapped in a plum tree, the narrator discussing various ways to bring it down—by threats, bribery, or offering it a plum.

Jack Horner, who pulls a "plum" out of his pie, has been interpreted by some scholars as having been a historical character who supposedly stole the deed of a beautiful estate from several destined for Henry VIII, a brave man indeed if this is true. The colloquialism "a plum," used of something desirable (and once referring specifically to the sum of £100,000), recalls the incident.

A well-known fortune-telling charm practiced by children involves counting plum-stones after dessert, while reciting, "Tinker, tailor, soldier, sailor, rich man, beggar man, poor man, thief" (or variants thereof). Whichever matched the last stone counted foretold a girl's future husband's occupation, or, in the case of a boy, revealed what he would be when grown.

Wild plums and **grapes** (though not, apparently, **cranberries**) were on the menu for the first American Thanksgiving in 1621.

To the British, "speaking with a plum in the mouth" or in "plummy tones" refers to either affecting an overly genteel accent or to the distinctively "rounded" accent of the upper class (see also **prune** below).

According to the Victorian flower language, plum trees represented independence.

The fruit has strong connections with Christmas, for plum cakes and pies were the ancestors of today's Christmas puddings and fruitcakes (see also plum broth in **prune**). "A plum-pudding voyage," however, appears to be a peculiarly American expression, referring to a voyage short enough to need only fresh provisions (including the mentioned item); thus, a "plum puddinger" was a ship (generally a whaler) which did not undertake long voyages.

**Peaches** were once called "Persian plums," and the **persimmon** was known as the "Virginian **date** plum."

A curious nineteenth-century expression, "to plum," meant to deliberately give someone erroneous information.

## Medicinal

Cherokee Indians used tea made from the bark of wild plums to treat bladder or kidney problems, and it was also used as a remedy for coughs.

Texans claim that chewing a plum-stone will prevent sunstroke.

## Mythological

The sage Lao-Tzu, author of the *Tao Te Ching*, was born under a plum tree (see also **cherry, date, olive**).

Plums grow in the Japanese Paradise (see also **apple, cherry, peach**).

An Australian Aboriginal legend tells of Najara, a spirit who entices men into the desert, where they lose their memories and wander about aimlessly. He was originally human, and a noted hunter, but was killed by a pack of wild dingoes under a plum tree, a favorite hunting place of his because emus eat wild plums (see also **raspberry**). Another Aboriginal legend tells of girls who ate plums, which turned them into devils.

# Prune

Prunes, dried plums, derived their name from the Latin *prunum*, meaning "plum."

### Ethnic

**Plum** broth, a Christmas delicacy particularly popular in the seventeenth century, was made of prunes, sugar, and wine.

Prunes form an alternative stuffing for the St. Martin's Day goose in Europe (see also **chestnut, gooseberry**).

Small figures made of prunes are traditional Christmas decorations in parts of Germany.

The prune's dried-up appearance has led to its unfortunate connection with spinsterhood, often with undertones of sourness or bitterness.

### Judaic

Prunes are a traditional filling for Hamantaschen, triangular pastries eaten during the festival of Purim (Hebrew, "lots"). Their name is commonly translated as "Haman's pockets," "ears," or "hats" (the latter referring to Haman's badge of office, and more recently taking on the meaning of repressive authority). It has, however, been suggested that the name is a corruption of the German *mohn-taschen* ("poppy pockets"), used of similar pastries with poppy-seed fillings.

As told in the Book of Esther, Haman plots to kill the Jews of Persia, casting purim (lots) to determine the best date for the slaughter. The wicked plot is foiled by Esther, wife of King Ahasuerus, and her cousin Mordecai, although not without much bloodshed. Haman is then hung on the fifty-cubit-high gallows on which he had intended to execute Mordecai, a fate which gave us the colloquialism, "hanging as high as Haman," used of someone meeting a fate he or she had intended for someone else. The story includes instructions that Purim be kept as a commemoration of deliverance (Esther 9:27-28), and it remains a popular festival with parties and dancing, which one rabbi described to me as a "Jewish Mardi Gras." In former times, an enemy of the Jewish people was sometimes called a "Haman." It has, alas, been rightly observed that while there are a multitude of Hamans, there is but a single Purim.

## Literary/Artistic

During the nineteenth century, young ladies were advised to practice saying phrases with words beginning with "P" as an aid to gaining an attractively shaped mouth. A popular phrase for this purpose, mentioned in Charles Dickens' *Little Dorrit* (1857), was "prunes and prisms" (see also **plum**).

## Symbolic Uses of the Plum (and/or Prune, where noted)

- Recalling Chinese symbolism of femininity, appropriate for Sweet Sixteen

- Recalling Japanese and Chinese symbolism of fidelity, appropriate for engagement; remarriage; wedding; wedding anniversary

- Recalling plum as a fruit of the Tree of Paradise, appropriate for funeral; wake

- Recalling medicinal use, appropriate for feast day of St. Blaise, invoked against throat ailments

- Recalling Texan sunstroke cure, appropriate for summer solstice

- Recalling Shichi-go-san, appropriate for third, fifth, and seventh birthdays

- Recalling connection with something desired, appropriate for good fortune

- Recalling early blooming's symbol of triumph, appropriate for first step; men's festivals'; new job; new venture; promotion; reaching goal; sports victories; women's festivals

- Recalling Victorian symbolism of independence, appropriate for Independence Day; Statehood Day

- Recalling Chinese symbolism of vigorous old age, appropriate for grandfather's birthday; grandmother's birthday; Grandparent's Day; retirement

- Recalling Chinese symbolism of strength, appropriate for get well soon; recovery

- Recalling role as winter friend, appropriate for winter solstice

- Recalling Japanese custom, appropriate for New Year's Day; New Year's Eve

- Recalling nursery rhyme about robins, appropriate for negotiation

- Recalling prune/plum's connection with diction, appropriate for first word

- Recalling prune's culinary use, appropriate for St. Martin's Day, and, recalling his role as patron of soldiers, also appropriate for Armed Forces Day; enlistment; military discharge

- Recalling connection with rain, appropriate for harvest festival; Kwanzaa; planting; Rogation Days; Thanksgiving; also, recalling tradition that rain on his feast day foretells forty more wet days, appropriate for St. Swithin's Day

- Recalling begging song, appropriate for All Souls Day

- Recalling colloquialism for short voyage, appropriate for bon voyage; launching; also appropriate for feast day of St. Clement, patron of sailors

# *Pomegranate*

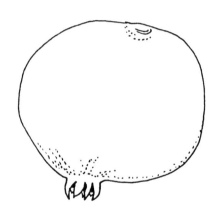

Thought to be a native of the North African region, the pomegranate's common name is derived from the Old French *pomme grenate*, loosely, "apple (with) many seeds." Its botanical name, *Punica grenatum*, describes the fruit succinctly, for it translates loosely as "red-purple many-seeded."

**Christian**   Pomegranates, probably the most pagan of all fruits, are not common in Christian art, but where they appear, they represent hope for eternal life, as in Joos van Cleve's *Virgin and Child with St. Joseph* (c. 1513) (see also **cherry, walnut**).

Their red flesh gives them the symbolism of suffering and sacrifice, making them emblematic of the Passion of Christ. Their multitude of seeds confers the meaning of unity, especially of the Church.

Pomegranates have been suggested as the fruit of the Tree of Knowledge (see also **apple, banana, fig, lemon, orange, quince, tomato**), and a European folktale has it that each of the fruits contains a seed from Eden.

Patterns of pomegranates have long been popular for material used for church furnishings.

**Ethnic**   The Hittite Law Code protected pomegranates, **apples,** and **grape**vines.

In many European countries, the pomegranate has long been regarded as an aphrodisiac, and it is said to dream of them foretells love. The Mesopotamians used them in love-spells; as a potent fertility symbol because of their many seeds, the fruit was eaten by brides in ancient Greece before the marriage was consummated. Turkish brides dropped a pomegranate on the floor during wedding celebrations; it was said the couple would have as many children as seeds spilt from the split fruit (see also **gourd** [in **melon**]). Chinese women wishing to bear children offered pomegranates to the gods (see also **coconut, fig, orange**).

The Persians regarded the fruit as an amulet against evil, and Egyptians flavored festive beers with its juice.

The Sicilian custom of using pomegranate wood rather than **hazel** for divining rods is an interesting link between stories of the underworld (see Mythological) and the underground water for which the diviner seeks.

The Romans called pomegranates "Carthaginian **apples**," after the fruit's supposed city of origin.

In the Victorian flower language, pomegranate blossoms represented elegance, but the fruit symbolized folly.

## Judaic

Representations of pomegranates decorated the Temple in Jerusalem (II Chronicles 3:16, 4:13).

Blue, scarlet, and purple pomegranates alternating with small golden bells were embroidered on the hem of the High Priest's robes (Exodus 28:33-34). The fruit on the hem has been interpreted several ways. They may have symbolized the Promised Land, where they grow in company with the **fig, grape**vine, and **olive** (Deuteronomy 8:8), or they may have represented divine beauty and glory. It has also been suggested that they were emblems of incorruptibility, from a tradition that they never decayed. Another possibility is that they represented triumph over pagan religions, to which the fruit was of particular importance (see Mythological).

Joel 1:7, 12, characterizes a desolated Israel as having fruitless pomegranate, **apples**, and **fig** trees, **date** palms, and **grape**vines.

A Hebrew folktale states that the pomegranate has 613 seeds, one each for the commandments in the five Books of Moses. In contemporary Israel, the fruit is eaten on Tu Bi-Shevat (see also **almond, fig, grape, olive**). Pomegranates often cap the rolls upon which the scroll of the Torah (Hebrew, "law") is wound.

Song of Songs 4:3 compares the temples of the beloved to the fruit.

**Literary/Artistic**

In pagan art in general, pomegranates represented death, sacrifice, the Earth or Mother Goddess, resurrection, fertility (from its numerous seeds), and the yoni (female genitalia; see also **almond, apricot, fig, grape**).

Balusters, vase-shaped supports for railings, derive their name from the French *balustre*, "pomegranate flower," after their shape.

In the modern Israeli military, *rimon* ("pomegranate") is slang for a hand-grenade (see also **pineapple**).

**Mythological**

The fruit was sacred to Tammuz, the vegetation god whose death and resurrection were mourned annually throughout the Mediterranean and Near Eastern countries.* Tammuz was the young lover of the Babylonian Mother Goddess Ishtar, but a jealous rival sent a boar which gored him to death, and pomegranates sprang from his blood. The Greeks equated Tammuz with Adonis, of whom a similar tale was told. He was loved by Aphrodite, goddess of love, who gave him into the care of the queen of the underworld, Persephone. She too fell in love with the boy and wanted him to stay with her. Zeus ruled that Adonis must spend six months with each goddess, but the youth was killed by a boar sent by Ares, god of war.

Statues of Hera, wife of Zeus, often showed her carrying a pomegranate, representing autumn, harvest, the death of the year, and resurrection.

---

\*  Women wailing Tammuz' death are mentioned in Ezekiel 8:14.

In Roman mythology, Pluto, ruler of the underworld, kidnapped Proserpine, daughter of the corn goddess Ceres. Neglecting her duties to nature, the goddess wandered the world, looking for her lost child. As nothing grew, humankind was thrown into a state of panic, and the council of gods ruled that, provided she had eaten nothing in the underworld, Proserpine could return to her mother. Alas, she had eaten six (in some versions, three) pomegranate seeds, and so had to spend the equivalent number of months each year underground (see also **apple**). This was held to account for the apparent death and resurrection of growing things each year, as her mother alternatively mourned and rejoiced at her daughter's absence or presence. Pomegranates have therefore been used not only as representing autumn but also spring (see also **almond, cherry, chestnut, peach**), when vegetation begins to grow again, and summer, when it is flourishing at its peak (see also **apple, melon, pear, strawberry**).

In Greek mythology, it was Persephone, Demeter's daughter, who was abducted by Hades, but the details remain the same. For this reason, pomegranate seeds were taboo food during the Thesmophoria (Greek, loosely, "bringing out" or "carrying out"), a women's festival held in October in honor of Demeter and her daughter, when offerings were thrown into a crevice or fissure, apparently emblematic of the underworld, and the remains of previous offerings removed. It has been suggested that the number of seeds consumed by Demeter's daughter represent the moon-phases between crop-planting and the appearance of the first seedlings (see also **fig, olive**).

In Phrygian legend, Attis, Cybele's lover, was conceived when Nana, daughter of the river god, placed a pomegranate (in some versions, an **almond**) in her lap or bosom. As a vegetation god, Attis was shown wearing a chaplet of pomegranates and pinecones and carrying fruit and corn (see also **pineapple**).

Pomegranates were sacred to the Egyptian goddess, Isis, and also had a funerary connection in that lotus, mandrake, and pomegranate blossoms were offered to the departed, and chaplets of the flowers were worn by mourners at funeral feasts.

Theban legend had it that a pomegranate tree grew from the tomb of Prince Menoeceus, who fulfilled an ancient prophecy by sacrificing himself to Ares, god of war, thus saving Thebes.

## Symbolic Uses of the Pomegranate

- Recalling Greek symbolism of autumn, appropriate for autumn equinox

- Recalling connection with femininity, appropriate for girl's birthday; women's festivals

- Recalling Victorian symbolism of folly, appropriate for April Fool's Day

- Recalling Christian symbolism of sacrifice, appropriate for Good Friday

- Recalling symbolism of unity, appropriate for Independence Day; peace celebration; reconciliation; Statehood Day

- Recalling connection with gods of vegetation, appropriate for Earth Day

- Recalling Christian symbolism of unity of Church, appropriate for baptism; confirmation; first eucharist; ordination; Pentecost

- Recalling role in Tu Bi-Shevat, appropriate for Arbor Day

- Recalling artistic symbolism of fertility, appropriate for baby shower

- Recalling Greek symbolism of harvest, appropriate for harvest festival; Kwanzaa; Thanksgiving

- Recalling Roman symbolism of spring and summer, appropriate for spring equinox; summer solstice

- Recalling Greek symbolism of death of year, appropriate for New Year's Day; New Year's Eve; winter solstice

- Recalling alleged aphrodisiac properties, appropriate for St. Valentine's Day

- Recalling pagan artistic symbolism of death, appropriate for anniversary of loss; birthday of departed; Memorial Day; remembering departed; requiem; wake

# Pumpkin

Like cucumbers, squash, and **melons**, pumpkins belong to the **gourd** family (see **melon**), and their common name reflects this, being derived from the Greek *pepon*, "edible gourd." Their botanical name, *Cucurbita maxima*, means "large gourd." Pumpkins are native to both Old and New Worlds.

Ethnic    A Parisian custom was for stall-holders in the markets to give exaggerated honor each autumn to a pumpkin decorated with a crown, but alas, King Pumpkin's reign did not last long, for he was subsequently cut up and auctioned off (see Literary/Artistic).

To the Chinese, pumpkins were the rulers of the garden.

New Britain tribes will not allow pigs to eat pumpkin rinds, for this, it is believed, will kill the animals.

Pumpkins are eaten for good fortune in Japan for Toji ("Winter Solstice"), especially in rural areas (see **citron**). Before harvesting the first fruits, the Kaffirs of South Africa ate a stew of pumpkin, corn, meat, and certain "magical" herbs. This rendered them "holy" enough to commence the harvest, a ceremony clearly acknowledging the sanctity of first fruits (see also **grape, raspberry**).

Hindu    Peanuts, rice, and pumpkins are popular offerings to Nepal's sacred monkeys, who are considered representatives of (and thus under the protection of) the monkey god Hanuman, also known as Hanumat (Sanskrit, "large-jawed"), who assisted Rama in his rescue of Sita by leaping from India to Ceylon and setting it on fire.

Literary/Artistic    The size of a pumpkin made it common at one time to refer to a person of self-importance as "some pumpkin"; from this arose "making a pumpkin (out) of," meaning a (usually humorous) glorification of an individual. Seneca had a similar meaning in mind when he described the deification of the Roman emperor Claudius as his "pumpkinification" (see Ethnic; see also **elderberry**).

Inquiring how the frost is "on the pumpkin" indicates that the speaker considers the person addressed to be a yokel or bumpkin. James Whitcomb Riley praises autumn in his *When the Frost Is on the Punkin* (1883).

In a survey of American terms of endearment in 1990, "pumpkin" appeared seventh on a list of ten. Things have therefore improved somewhat, since "pumpkin head" was used of New England residents because, it was said, their hair was cut around a pumpkin-shaped bowl, if not an actual pumpkin shell.

In nursery lore, Cinderella's coach was originally a pumpkin, though not, it is to be hoped, the Great Pumpkin of *Peanuts* comic-strip fame, or part of Jack Pumpkinhead, one of the residents of L. Frank Baum's *Oz*. The nursery rhyme about Peter the pumpkin-eater, who is unable to keep a wife until he puts her into a pumpkin shell, has rather sinister undertones, given the pumpkin's connection with the dead.

## Mythological

September sacrifices to Chicomecoatl, Mexican goddess of maize, were made in temples whose floors were piled high with pumpkins, peppers, maize, roses, and vegetable and fruit seeds. It was thought that the blood spilt upon these revitalized all plants, ensuring excellent harvests as well as honoring the goddess.

In America, pumpkins represent the earth's bounty at Thanksgiving but have a more sinister connotation at Halloween. Jack-o'-Lanterns have been connected with the Celtic cult of the head, which was regarded as the seat of the soul. Halloween has also been connected with the Celtic festival Samhain, which was celebrated annually on November 1 and marked their new year. The night before was considered a time of great danger, when spirits returned to this world and all manner of strange things happened. It was therefore only wise to make offerings to the departed to appease them, and it was not uncommon for burial places to be illuminated all night. Similarly, graveyards are lit today on the night of All Souls in countries as geographically distant as northern Europe and South America.

It has also been suggested that Jack-o'-Lanterns represent harvest spirits.

## Symbolic Uses of the Pumpkin

- Recalling Thanksgiving symbolism of earth's bounty, appropriate for Earth Day; harvest festival; Kwanzaa; Thanksgiving

- Recalling colloquialism for New England tonsorial custom, appropriate for first haircut

- Recalling traditional symbolism, appropriate for Halloween

- Recalling literary symbolism of glorification, appropriate for press conference; promotion; reaching goal; recognition award

- Recalling Japanese custom, appropriate for winter solstice

- Recalling Kaffir custom, appropriate for first fruits

# Quince

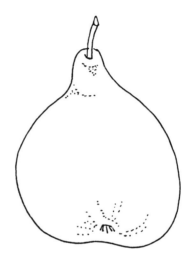

Native to the Central Asian area, the strongly flavored quince is much used as a grafting tree. Its common name is derived from the Middle English "quynce," the plural of "quyn" or "coyn," ultimately derived from the Latin *cydonium*, "quince." Its botanical name, *Cydonia oblonga*, is self-descriptive, meaning, loosely, "quince (with) flattened end." It has also been connected with Cydonia (present-day Canea) in Crete, where the fruit supposedly originated and which in Classical times was famous for its quince orchards.

**Christian**  Quinces share the symbolism of the **apple**, and it is probably for this reason that they have been suggested as the fruit of the Tree of Knowledge (see also **apple, banana, fig, lemon, orange, pomegranate, tomato**). They also represent redemption and resurrection, though, curiously, not temptation.

**Ethnic**  Ancient Greeks considered quinces a particularly potent fertility symbol and served them to the bride at wedding feasts.

The *samisen*, a three-stringed Japanese instrument, is traditionally made of oak or quince wood. With chorus, drums, and flutes, it forms part of the accompaniment for No theatrical performances. At one time, the samisen's squarish body was covered with cat and dog skins, and a monument to these unfortunate animals was erected on Mount Minobu in Japan some years ago.

The Quinces in Comfit eaten at the coronation banquet of Henry IV (1399) were candied, a popular, though expensive, sweetmeat of the time. It may be coincidence that one of the fruit's symbolisms is luxury (see also **chestnut, grapefruit**).

In modern floral usage, quince blossoms in a bride's bouquet represent hopes for marital happiness.

**Literary/Artistic**  It is said that the grateful citizens of Orleans presented Joan of Arc with quince preserves (a local delicacy) when she broke their siege in 1429.

In nursery lore, Edward Lear's Owl and Pussycat dine on quinces and mince (the British term for ground beef) after their sea voyage, as described in his 1871 poem.

**Medicinal**   Medieval herbalists used preparations from quinces for eye lotions.

**Mythological**   Greek gardeners offered quinces, **apples, figs, grapes**, and vegetables to Priapus, god of male generative powers, in order to obtain his protection for their crops.

## Symbolic Uses of the Quince

- Recalling use for musical instruments, appropriate for feast day of St. Cecilia, patron of musicians

- Recalling the Owl and Pussycat's meal, appropriate for bon voyage

- Recalling modern floral symbolism of marital good fortune, appropriate for remarriage; wedding; wedding anniversary

- Recalling Greek custom, appropriate for feast day of St. Fiacre, patron of gardeners

- Recalling medicinal use, appropriate for feast day of St. Lucy, invoked against eye ailments

- Recalling French gift, appropriate for feast day of St. Joan of Arc

- Recalling Christian symbolism of redemption/resurrection, appropriate for All Souls Day; Easter Sunday; funeral

- Recalling use as grafting tree, appropriate for adoption

# *Raspberry*

According to legend, the Olympian gods went berrying on Mount Ida and there discovered the raspberry. This is recalled in the fruit's botanical name, *Rubus idaeus*, "bramble bush (of) Ida." Its common name is derived variously from the raspiness of its canes or its similarity in color to *raspeit* or *raspei*, a French wine popular during the period 1400-1500. At one time the raspberry was known as the "raspis" and is mentioned as such in early herbals. The raspberry is native to both Old and New Worlds.

**Christian**      In Christian art, the raspberry was a symbol of kindness because its red juice recalled the blood of the heart, whence flows kind thoughts and deeds. It was sometimes, albeit uncommonly, used as a Marian symbol (see also **almond, apple, cherry, lemon, olive, strawberry, walnut**).

**Ethnic**      Raspberry shoots were considered a particular delicacy among the Native American tribes of the northwest. The first of the season were honored in a ceremony in which the tribe stood in a circle while prayers were offered to the soul of the fruit, asking that there be many shoots to gather. The first, having been prepared in a new bowl, were then distributed to all. This ceremony recognizes the sanctity of first fruits (see also **grape, pumpkin**).

One tribe in the Philippines formerly hung raspberry canes outside their dwellings to snare returning souls, thus protecting the bereaved family.

Raspberries are not good "travelers," and thus are emblematic of fragility. They also represent sorrow or remorse (see also **blackberry, elderberry**).

**Literary/Artistic**      An old name for the raspberry was "hyndberry" or "hindberry," from the folktale that deer ate the berries of the wild fruit (see also **plum**).

The verbal "raspberry" or "Bronx cheer," indicating contempt or derision, is softened somewhat in "razzing," good-natured ribbing, a meaning which inspired the Golden Raspberries, or "Razzies," awarded each year to the worst films by the Golden Raspberry Award Foundation.

## Medicinal

English herbalists prescribed raspberry tea for pregnant women, believing it ensured an easy delivery; Cherokee women drank infusions of the fruit during labor for the same reason. This connection with birth gives raspberries the secondary symbolism of relief from pain (see also **cherry**).

During the seventeenth century, raspberry gargles were commonly recommended for throat ailments. Folk medicine claims that rubbing rheumatic joints with raspberry canes cures, or at least alleviates, the pain (see also **chestnut, walnut**).

# Symbolic Uses of the Raspberry

- Recalling Marian symbolism, appropriate for Marian festivals

- Recalling old name of "hindberry," appropriate for feast days of Sts. Francis, patron of animals, Giles (who according to legend saved a hind), and Hubert (whose emblem is a stag)

- Recalling Native American custom, appropriate for first fruits

- Recalling herbal use for easy delivery, appropriate for baby shower; also appropriate for feast day of Sts. Anne, patron of women in labor, and Raymond Nonnatus, patron of expectant mothers and midwives

- Recalling Christian symbolism of kindness, appropriate for adoption; birth; family/general birthday; Father's Day; Friendship Day; Grandparent's Day; Mother's Day; peace celebration; remarriage; Sweetest Day; wedding

- Recalling medicinal use, appropriate for feast day of St. Blaise, invoked against throat ailments

- Recalling symbolism of relief from pain, apprpriate for get well soon; recovery; also appropriate for feast days of Sts. Luke, patron of physicians, Camillus, patron of nurses and the sick, and saints invoked against illnesses

- Recalling symbolism of remorse, appropriate for feast day of St. Mary Magdalen

- Recalling connection with derision, appropriate for divorce; separation; (on a humorous note) Over-the- Hill (40th) birthday

# *Strawberry*

Native to both Old and New Worlds, the strawberry belongs to the genus *Fragaria*, related to the Latin *fragum*, "strawberry." Its common name derives from the straw placed around it to protect its delicate berries.

**Christian**    In Christian art, flowers and berries shown together symbolize righteousness and spiritual merit, while the plant's trefoil leaves represent the Trinity. The strawberry has also been used to symbolize Mary (for other Marian symbolism, see also **almond, apple, cherry, lemon, olive, raspberry, walnut**).

Archbishop Hugh Latimer coined the phrase "strawberry preacher" in 1549 to describe clerics who, like the berry, appear but once a year and then only briefly.

An unlikely European legend has it that John the Baptist lived on the fruit.

**Ethnic**    In parts of Germany, it is still the custom to eat strawberries and drink woodruff-flavored wine on May Day.

Like **melons**, the berry has long been connected with summer, and the traditional American name for June's full moon is the "Strawberry Moon" (see also **apple, blackberry, chestnut, pear, pomegranate**).

Strawberry leaves decorate the coronets of British marquis, earls, and dukes, inspiring a nineteenth-century term for a fortune-hunter: "going hunting strawberry leaves."

In the Victorian flower language, the berry stood for perfection (see also **pineapple**) and for sweetness in life and character. It also represented modesty, from the way the berries "hide" under their leaves.

In Sweden, traditional fare for Midsummer's Day includes strawberries.

Following the traditional culinary last fling before Lent, it was the custom in Scotland to add strawberries (if available) to the Shrove Tuesday crowdie, a rich porridge made with sherry and cream.

Bavarian folklore claims that it is possible to get into the good graces of fairy-folk with a gift of strawberries.

Elizabeth I likened shallow display to the baskets of unscrupulous strawberry sellers, who put the biggest and most luscious fruit on top, hiding the smaller, inferior berries beneath.

The Germans call the fruit *erdbeere*, "earth (or ground) berry."

## Literary/Artistic

In pagan art, the three-pointed leaves of the strawberry represented the three-fold Earth or Mother Goddess.

In *The Compleat Angler* (1653), Izaak Walton quotes a contemporary's remark that "Doubtless God could have made a better berry, but doubtless God never did."

An old nursery rhyme mentions someone asking how many strawberries may be found in the sea, to which the answer is as many herrings as may be found growing in a wood. Another rhyme gives a version of the Babes in the Wood story, at the close of which a charitable robin covers the dead children with strawberry leaves, recalling the Norse legend mentioned below (see Mythological).

In his *Essay on Gardens* (c. 1625), Francis Bacon names plants he considers best of all for perfuming a garden, listing dying strawberry leaves third (after violets and musk-roses), an early tribute to the plant's fragrance.

## Mythological

The fruit has connections with Freyja, Norse goddess of love, and one of their legends tells of children's spirits entering the afterlife hidden in strawberries taken to heaven by Odin's compassionate wife, Frigga (see Literary/Artistic).

## Symbolic Uses of the Strawberry

- Recalling Christian symbolism of spiritual merit, appropriate for baptism; confirmation; first eucharist; pilgrimage

- Recalling Marian symbolism, appropriate for Marian festivals

- Recalling Victorian symbolism of modesty, appropriate for Sweet Sixteen

- Recalling strawberry leaves' symbolism of Trinity, appropriate for Trinity Sunday

- Recalling European legend, appropriate for feast day of St. John the Baptist

- Recalling German custom, appropriate for May Day

- Recalling Victorian symbolism of sweetness in life/character, appropriate for congratulations; Friendship Day; good fortune; milestones; reaching goal; recognition award; reconciliation; retirement; sports victories; Sweetest Day; wedding anniversary

- Recalling connection with kindly love, appropriate for baby shower; bridal shower; engagement; remarriage; wedding; also appropriate for St. Valentine's Day

- Recalling connection with June, appropriate for Midsummer's Day; Midsummer's Eve; summer solstice

- Recalling pagan artistic symbolism of Earth/Mother Goddess, appropriate for women's festivals

- Recalling Norse legend and nursery rhyme, appropriate for Holy Innocents Day

- Recalling Scottish culinary use, appropriate for Shrove Tuesday

- Recalling lunar connection, appropriate for full moon

# *Tomato*

The tomato originated in South America, its common name being derived from its Nahuatl name, *tomatl*. Its botanical name, *Lycopersicum esculentum*, means "edible wolf **peach**." The term may refer to either the lesser flavor of the tomato compared to the **peach** or to the tomato's more aggressive color.

**Christian**  European folklore suggests the tomato as the fruit of Tree of Knowledge, and the Old German name for tomato, *Paradies apfel* ("Paradise **apple**"), recalls this tradition (see also **apple, banana, fig, lemon, orange, pomegranate, quince**).

**Ethnic**  The tomato did not arrive in Europe until the early 1600s. A member of the nightshade family, it was originally considered highly poisonous (see also **peach**), although grown for ornamental use. It later gained a reputation for being a powerful aphrodisiac, earning the nickname "love **apple**," also applied to mandrakes and eggplants, which supposedly shared these alleged properties. In the case of the tomato, however, the nickname is also connected with a misinterpretation of the French *pomme d'or*, "**apple** of gold" (the first tomatoes arriving from the New World were reportedly the yellow-skinned variety), as *pomme d'amour*, "**apple** of love." *Pomme d'amour* is currently used of the tomato in France, and, like the **blackberry** and **fig**, the tomato appropriately symbolizes lust.

Because of its origin, the tomato is emblematic of the New World.

**Hindu**  Yogis believed tomatoes in the diet exerted a calming effect, particularly on the mental processes (**dates** were also considered to have this property).

## Symbolic Uses of the Tomato

- Recalling connection with the New World, appropriate for Columbus Day; new immigrant; also appropriate for feast day of St. Frances Cabrini, patron of immigrants

- Recalling yogis' belief, appropriate for religious retreat

- Recalling alleged aphrodisiac properties, appropriate for St. Valentine's Day

# NUTS

# Almond

Almonds are thought to have originated in Asia. They belong to the genus *Prunus*, "**plum tree**," and their common name is derived from the Middle English "almande" via the Latin *amygdala*, "almond."

**Christian**     Some icons show Christ surrounded by almonds because the nut represents the womb. In Christian art, the almond was used to symbolize Mary, a practice particularly favored in central Italy (for other Marian symbolism, see also **apple, cherry, lemon, olive, raspberry, strawberry, walnut**).

A French legend concerning St. Honoratus of Arles, who lived on an island, relates that his sister wished to visit him, but he would only see her when the almond trees bloomed. She prayed for assistance, and an almond tree on the shore blossomed year-round.

**Ethnic**     Romans showered newlyweds with almonds as a fertility charm. A modern European custom is to give female guests at weddings a bag of five sugared almonds, representing children, happiness, romance, good health, and fortune.

The Romans considered the almond, like the **hazel, walnut**, and other nuts, to represent children.

In the East, the nut was emblematic of the yoni (female genitalia; see also **apricot, fig, grape, pomegranate**), while the sweetness of the kernel is transferred symbolically to the character. Almonds also represent amorous ardor and marital bliss.

The Chinese considered almond blossoms to represent feminine beauty (see also **cherry, peach, plum**). In western symbolism, almond blossoms meant overcoming sorrow, while in the Victorian flower language, a branch of blooming almond meant hope.

In Germany, almond-paste animals, hearts, stars, and so on are popular Christmas treats; similar sweetmeats are given to Dutch children on St. Nicholas' Eve. In Sweden, cinnamon-flavored rice pudding, with an almond hidden in it, is eaten at Christmas; whoever finds the nut is guaranteed good fortune for a year. A similar custom in northern Germany rewards the finder with a small gift.

Almond cookies are a popular wedding food in Greece. The traditional almond paste and royal icing of British wedding cakes is said to symbolize the intermingled sweetness and bittersweetness of the couple's new life together. Almond paste alone covers the traditional British Mothering Sunday Simnel Cake, connecting the nut with motherhood.

A Portuguese legend from the Algarve tells of a princess from the north married to a Moor. She pines for her snowy homeland, so he plants many almond trees which, when they bloom in February, look as if they are covered in snow, thus cheering the homesick princess.

An old Romanian contraceptive measure was to carry roasted almonds on the person, presumably because roasting counteracted the nut's traditional connections with fertility, and by extension, prevented conception.

Like all nuts, almonds represent knowledge, particularly in Celtic countries.

## Judaic

Exodus 25:33 specifies that the golden candlesticks for the Tabernacle were to have almond-shaped bowls. Ornamental pieces of crystal attached to candlesticks are still called almonds.

Numbers 17 tells of the laying-up of the rods of tribal elders in the Tabernacle, God having declared that divine approval will be signified by the flowering of one rod (v. 5). Next day, Aaron's rod is found to have blossomed and borne almonds (v. 8), thus emphasizing his authority and giving the nut the symbolism of divine approval. It has been suggested that this incident also had a certain propagandic value to the Tribe of Levi, to which Aaron belonged (see also **date**).

Jeremiah 1:11 records that the prophet sees an almond branch. By tradition, the almond is first to flower in spring (see Mythological), and its Hebrew name, *shaked*, may be translated as "watchful." The tree is sometimes called the "watch tree" for this reason. This meaning is punned upon in verse 12, when the Lord says that God's word will be watched and seen to be performed. (In the Authorized Version, the translation says that God's word will be hastened and performed, thus losing some of the nuances of the passage.) The passage has been interpreted as a symbol of the Lord's watching over the world and as a promise to also watch over Jeremiah and the Chosen People. It is from this that the almond, although not among the Seven Species of Israel, has become popular for celebrations of Tu Bi-Shevat (see also **fig, grape, olive, pomegranate**).

Cakes made from almond flour are popular for Passover among Ashkenazic Jews (see also **coconut**), while North African Jews serve cakes of almond, honey, and spices for the same festivity.

## Medicinal

Because of their similarity in shape, the tonsils were once known colloquially as "the almonds of the throat."

According to a sixteenth-century herbal, almond and **peach** trees flower together in the spring, the first trees to do so and thus emblematic of the season (see also **cherry, chestnut, pomegranate**).

Mythological

In Greek myth, Phyllis ("leafy") of Thrace grieved so much when her lover Demophon did not return from Troy (or, some say, was delayed in Athens) that she pined away and was turned into an almond tree. When Demophon finally returned, he embraced the tree, which burst into blossom, and the Greeks therefore said that this was why the almond is first to flower in spring. From this, almonds acquired their traditional symbolism of vigilance and watchfulness (see also **hazel**; see Judaic).*

According to a cult from Asia Minor, the almond tree sprang from the blood of Cybele, who was originally hermaphrodite. Nana, daughter of the river god, gathered almonds of this tree, and after sitting with them in her lap (in some versions, in her bosom), gave birth to Attis, whose fate it was to be both Cybele's son and lover (see also **pineapple, pomegranate**). The Phrygians of Asia Minor were Cybele's chief devotees, regarding the almond as Father of Everything. Almonds also symbolized Cybele, whose rites were particularly savage and whose worship was eventually banned in Rome.

It was the custom to eat almonds and **walnuts** during festivals honoring Metis (Greek, "wise counsel"), first wife of Zeus. According to legend, Zeus swallowed Metis whilst she was pregnant, but the baby, Athene, goddess of wisdom, was born by springing fully grown from Zeus' head. It is probable that this story relates to the walnut's traditional symbolism, shared with other nuts, of knowledge and wisdom.

---

\* A similar story is told of Carya (see **walnut**).

## *Symbolic Uses of the Almond*

- Recalling Judaic symbolism of hope for Divine approval, appropriate for confirmation; first eucharist; ordination; pilgrimage

- Recalling Roman symbolism of children, appropriate for children's birthdays; Children's Day; Holy Innocents Day

- Recalling Marian symbolism, appropriate for Christmas; Epiphany; Marian festivals

- Recalling French legend, appropriate for feast day of St. Honoratus of Arles; also appropriate for family reunions

- Recalling symbolism of sweetness of character, appropriate for Sweetest Day

- Recalling Phrygian symbolism of fatherhood, appropriate for father's birthday; Father's Day; father-in-law's birthday; grandfather's birthday; Grandparent's Day; men's festivals; recalling nickname of "Father of His Country," Washington's birthday

- Recalling common symbolism of knowledge, appropriate for beginning kindergarten/college/school; commencement; graduation; reaching adulthood

- Recalling symbolism of marital bliss, appropriate for bridal shower; remarriage; wedding

- Recalling colloquialism for tonsils, appropriate for feast day of St. Blaise, invoked against throat ailments

- Recalling connection with spring, appropriate for spring equinox

- Recalling role in Tu Bi-Shevat, appropriate for Arbor Day

- Recalling symbolism of overcoming sorrow, appropriate for birthday of departed; celebration of life; Memorial Day; remembering departed; requiem

# *Chestnut*

## *with notes on Horse Chestnut*

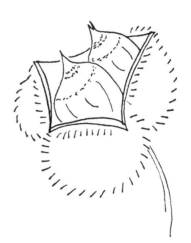

Native to both Old and New Worlds, the chestnut's botanical name is *Castanea sativa*, "cultivated chestnut." Its common name is derived from the Middle English "chesteine-nut."

**Buddhist**  During the wanderings of the priest Kobo-Daishi, founder of the Shingon branch of Buddhism, he acknowledged hospitality (or the lack of it) with blessings (or the reverse). In the case of the chestnut, which provided him with food during a time of shortage, he rewarded the tree by declaring henceforth it would bear nuts twice or even thrice a year (see also **peach, pear**; for a similar story about Elijah, see **melon**).

**Christian**  In early Christian art, chestnuts represented chastity and the rejection of temptation because their sweetness, surrounded by thorns, remains untouched.

In northern areas of Italy, chestnuts are left for the departed on All Saints Eve, and the nut is traditional fare in Galicia, Spain, for All Saints Day, and in Tuscany, Italy, for St. Simon's Day.

**Ethnic**  It was once the custom of Abruzzi, Italy, to burn a figure of Carnival at the beginning of Lent, as chestnuts were thrown to the crowd (see also **gourd** [in **melon**]).

Chestnut stuffing accompanies the St. Martin's Day goose in many European countries, especially Germany and Sweden (see also **gooseberry, prune** [in **plum**]).

Chestnuts were a popular Christmas treat in the nineteenth century and remain so today.

Chestnuts are a popular New Year food in Japan because their written name includes a character meaning, loosely, "to gain ascendancy over." The chestnut therefore symbolizes success or victory (see Ethnic entry in **horse chestnut**).

A Scottish love-charm is to place two chestnuts on the fire. If they burst, or burn together, the lovers are true; if not, the reverse applies. There is some irony, therefore, in the colloquialism, "pulling one's chestnuts out the fire," meaning a narrow escape, especially one due to quick-thinking action on the part of the person in danger.

It was a pleasant nineteenth-century custom in one town in Hertfordshire, England, to visit local parks to view the chestnut blossoms on Chestnut Sunday, early in spring. Thus the tree may represent the season (see also **almond, cherry, peach, pomegranate**).

Chestnuts were once known as "Trees of Life" in the mountains of southern France, from their many uses, both of nut and wood; in the sixteenth century, payment for services rendered was often made in chestnuts or the wherewithal with which to grow them.

Roman legions marched on rations which included sweet chestnut flour, a similar type of which was commonly used in England for breadmaking up to the last century.

In the Creek Indian calendar, September and October were called "Little Chestnut" and "Big Chestnut" months respectively (see also **blackberry, strawberry**).

The Native American chestnut, *Castanea dentata* (loosely, "chestnut [with] sawtooth leaves," from the shape of its foliage), is now virtually extinct, having fallen prey to blight.

British folklore claims that carrying a chestnut prevents rheumatism (a belief mentioned in one of O. Henry's short stories), while in Germany it is said to ease a backache (see also **raspberry, walnut**).

To the Victorians, chestnuts represented both luxury (see also **grapefruit, quince**) and a plea for justice (see also **pear**).

Judaic    Genesis 30 relates that Laban agrees that all spotted or speckled livestock will become Jacob's property as payment for his services. Jacob practices what is clearly an imitative magic charm involving rods of chestnut, **hazel**, and poplar, cut so that the inner white shows. When strong, healthy livestock come to drink, Jacob places these rods in the troughs so that their offspring will be spotted or speckled and thus become his. When weaker livestock drink, however, he does not do this; thus over time this selective breeding process obtains him a large flock of superior animals, while Laban's herd is of poorer quality.

Referring to the glory of Assyria, Ezekiel 31:8 compares its beauty to chestnut trees.

Literary/Artistic    The colloquialism "an (old) chestnut," used of a story told numerous times, has been traced to a character in a nineteenth-century tale who interrupts someone telling an anecdote about a cork-tree to observe that it had, in fact, been a chestnut tree—a fact known to him because he had already heard the story twenty-seven times.

# Horse Chestnut

The botanical name of the horse chestnut is *Aesculus hippocastanum* (loosely, "acorn-bearing horse chestnut"). It is native to Asia and Europe. Its common name, John Gerard's 1597 herbal suggests (apparently quoting a work published some fifty years earlier), is derived from its use in eastern countries as a cure for equine coughs and chest ailments.

**Ethnic**

The horse chestnut is not edible but is commonly used by British children for the game of conkers. A nut is threaded on a string and swung against other nuts similarly threaded, the object being to smash all opposing conkers and emerge the winner or conqueror—hence the name of the game. Horse chestnuts can therefore symbolize victory (see Ethnic entry in **chestnut**). The British colloquialism, "conking out," meaning to die and usually (though not always) applied to inanimate objects, may well be derived from this game.

To the French, the horse chestnut is the *Marron d'Inde*, "Chestnut of India," a reminder of Gerard's herbal comment, which connects it with eastern countries.

Europeans say that throwing horse chestnuts into a river renders the fish unconscious, making them easier to catch.

## *Symbolic Uses of the Chestnut (and/or Horse Chestnut, where noted)*

- Recalling Christian symbolism of chastity/rejection of temptation, appropriate for confirmation; first communion; pilgrimage; remarriage; wedding

- Recalling Victorian symbolism of justice, appropriate for Election Day; jury duty; taking office

- Recalling British spring custom, appropriate for Rogation Days; spring equinox

- Recalling Spanish and Italian customs, appropriate for All Saints Day; All Saints Eve

- Recalling Japanese custom, appropriate for New Year's Day; New Year's Eve

- Recalling Tuscan custom, appropriate for St. Simon's Day

- Recalling fate of Native American chestnut, appropriate as a symbol of endangered species and, by extension, Earth Day

- Recalling culinary use, appropriate for St. Martin's Day and, recalling his role as patron of soldiers, appropriate for Armed Forces Day; enlistment; military discharge

- Recalling Creek Indian connection with September, appropriate for autumn equinox

- Recalling Italian custom, appropriate for Lent; Shrove Tuesday

- Recalling connection with fish, appropriate for feast days of Sts. Andrew and Peter, James and John

- Recalling colloquialism referring to oft-told stories, appropriate for family/college/high school reunions

- Recalling horse chestnut's symbolism of victory, appropriate for sports victories

# Coconut

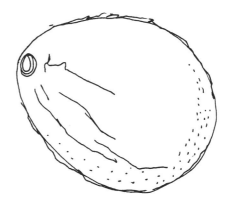

Perhaps the most useful of nuts (providing food, drink, fibers for clothing, matting, nets and ropes—and the wherewithal for a potent wine), coconuts are native to the Indo-Pacific area. It is thought that Portuguese explorers returning from India brought back the first to Europe, hence its old nickname of "Indian nut." Its common name is derived from the Portuguese *cocar*, meaning, loosely, "make an odd face," from the similarity of the markings on the coconut base to a face. Its botanical name, *Cocos nucifera*, meaning, loosely, "face-nut-bearing," reflects this tradition.

**Christian**   Easter celebrations among the Kekchi villagers of Belize include carrying a statue of Christ through the streets in a small palm-leaf house on Easter Sunday.

**Ethnic**   Like the **banana**, the coconut has connotations of exotic lands and faraway places. It is said to be the most widely consumed nut globally.

The Dyaks of Borneo magically transferred infant souls to coconut shells for the first year of a child's life, the better to protect the fragile spirit, which might otherwise come to harm in the child's body.

It was believed among pagan Melanesians that to break a taboo brought madness which would cause the violator to kill himself, either by self-starvation or by jumping from atop a coconut palm.

In some cultures, the coconut's resemblance to the human head made it an acceptable sacrificial substitute for the real thing (see Mythological).

Fiji Islanders planted a breadfruit tree or coconut palm when a baby was born, believing the infant's fate was bound up in that of the tree (see also **apple, pear**).

In Malaya, offerings of sugar and coconut were made to the Rice Mother, the sheaf from which ears were taken to make the Rice Child, an important part of the harvest celebration. Coconuts were also part of a new mother's post-natal diet for the first three days after birth (see also **banana, date, orange**). Among the Bajaus people of the Philippines, the afterbirth is buried in a coconut shell on the shore.

Warriors from the Cook Islands wear flower-pot-like head-dresses made from sennit (coconut fiber rope), while their counterparts in Tonga adorn themselves with narrow combs made from coconut leaf ribs.

Funeral rites on Malekula in the New Hebrides include the appearance of men completely covered in fern leaves, with sticks holding pieces of coconut protruding from the foliage; mourners eat the coconut in order to communicate with spirits.

Because the coconut palm provided such an abundance of useful things, the Wanika people of eastern Africa regarded destroying one as tantamount to murdering a parent, who provides life's necessities for a child.

In India, ships are named by breaking a coconut (rather than a bottle of champagne) on them, and, during the monsoon period, coconuts are offered to the sea gods to calm the winds.

## Hindu

In India, coconuts were called *Sri-phala* (Sanskrit, "Sri's fruit"), Sri being an incarnation of Lakshmi, goddess of prosperity.

The nut is considered sacred, and it was formerly said that only those of the priestly caste should plant them.

Blessed coconuts were given to women desiring a family (see also **fig, orange, pomegranate**).

With their womb-like shape and milk, coconuts also symbolize rebirth, and Hindus today often include them in offerings made upon the anniversary of a death.

Sarasvati, goddess of learning and the arts and sciences, is usually represented as a four-armed woman holding a drum, a necklace, a flower, and a book made of palm leaves, the latter item representing her love of all learning.

The three indentations on the base of a coconut represent the three eyes of Shiva, and the nut is therefore particularly sacred to his devotees.

| | |
|---|---|
| **Islamic** | A favorite dish for Eid al-Fitr (Arabic, loosely, "Festival of the end of the Fast") is noodles prepared with coconut, sugar, and milk. Eid al-Fitr marks the end of the daylight fasting during the holy month of Ramadan. |
| **Judaic** | Coconut cakes are popular desserts for Passover among the Ashkenazic Jews (see also **almond**). |
| **Literary/Artistic** | Colloquially, exclaiming, "*That's* how the milk got into the coconut!" indicates a revelation. |
| **Mythological** | In Java, a ritual honoring the sea goddess involves dipping opened coconuts into the sea, pouring mixed coconut milk and seawater over the hands, and offering prayers. |

The Burmese formerly offered coconuts and bread to rain spirits residing in tamarind trees.

In Indonesia, Upu-Lera ("Mr. Sun") was represented by lamps of coconut leaves hung in dwellings and on his sacred **fig** trees. Offerings were made to these lamps when Upu-Lera made his annual visit to the world to fertilize plants and animals.

Pacific cultures regarded the coconut as symbolizing both love and knowledge, having sprung forth from the head of the eel god Tuna (the Maori word for the species), who was sacrificed to redeem humankind. Thus, to eat the nut was to partake of the divine body. In addition, the unripe nuts of the two species growing on the islands represented heaven and the underworld.

A Sri Lankan legend relates that the first coconut palm appeared where the head of a court astrologer had been buried, he having predicted the day a good one for planting. Another island tale disagrees, however, stating that the palm grew where the severed head of a loathsome monster had been interred (appropriately, in western slang, the head is often referred to as a coconut, usually shortened to "nut"; see Ethnic).

## *Symbolic Uses of the Coconut*

- Recalling connection with food and shelter, appropriate for housewarming; new home

- Recalling connection with Lakshmi, appropriate for good fortune; new venture; reaching goal

- Recalling connection with birth, appropriate for adoption; birth

- Recalling coconut's many uses and thus connection with abundance, appropriate for Earth Day; harvest festival; Kwanzaa; Thanksgiving

- Recalling Hindu symbolism of rebirth, appropriate for funeral; remembering departed; requiem; wake

- Recalling connection with exotic lands, appropriate for bon voyage; leaving home

- Recalling Indian custom, appropriate for launching

# Hazel

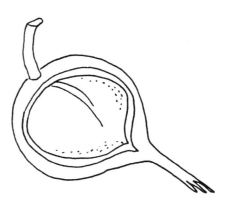

The hazel gives its name to the genus *Corylus*, "hazel tree," from the Latin *corulus*, meaning the same. Its common name is derived from the Middle English "hasel." Hazels are native to both Old and New Worlds.

**Christian**   The nuts of the cultivated hazel are called filberts; a medieval writer considered them the most wholesome of all nuts. The name is derived from the tradition that they ripen about the time of St. Philibert's Day in August, though some have connected the name with that of Phyllis, who, according to Greek myth, was turned into an **almond** tree.

**Ethnic**   Hazel leaves decorated the Tree Spirit featured in Whit Monday ceremonies in Bohemia. Accompanied by attendants, the Tree Spirit rode to the village square, in which a May tree and small hut had been erected. After celebrations which included criticizing all the village women, the Spirit was chased by his attendants and, if caught, was beaten with wooden swords or hazel rods and then "beheaded."

Some European traditions speak of souls enclosed in hazel shells (see also **walnut**).

Hazel twigs were once substituted in France for the willow rods commonly used for "beating boundaries," the annual progression around the parish (or town) limits during which the boundaries were thrashed. It was said this helped the townspeoples' memories.

A fifteenth-century English charm which supposedly granted invisibility involved carrying a hazel rod.

In medieval times, love-cakes (thought to act as an aphrodisiac) were made from ingredients which included fern-seed gathered on Midsummer's Eve. Because the fern was considered a fairy plant, to touch one was to court disaster, so the seeds were obtained by shaking the plant with a hazel twig.

In eastern Europe, hazel wood is the choice for cradles, although birch is also recommended (see also **elderberry**). Curiously, biers of both hazel and birch carried the English and Scottish dead from the Battle of Otterburn (1388), according to the anonymous *Ballad of Chevy Chase* (c. 1550); perhaps this was an oblique reference to their rebirth, if not coincidence.

Fittingly, it is said that a large crop of hazel nuts forecasts numerous births the following year, and, like the **almond, walnut**, and other nuts, hazels are an emblem of childhood.

Hazel wood was traditionally preferred for kindling (English bakers in particular favored it) and was therefore considered sacred to fire gods (see also **fig, pear**).

In Europe, the tree's connection with water made it the wood of choice for diviner's rods (the best were said to be those cut on St. John's Eve), which also had the ability, so it was said, to find buried treasure and murder victims (see also **pomegranate**).

## Judaic

Genesis 30 relates that Jacob increased his livestock by means of a charm involving rods of poplar, hazel, and **chestnut.**

## Literary/Artistic

In his restored Druid Tree Alphabet, Robert Graves gives hazel as the tree of the ninth month, beginning August 5 and representing the letter "C" (see also **blackberry, elderberry, grape**).

Hazels also symbolized lovers, and in one version of the story of Tristan and Isolde, hazel and honeysuckle grow from their graves and intertwine together (see also **grape**).

Reference is made in Shakespeare's *Romeo and Juliet* (1594) to the fairy Queen Mab's hazel-nut chariot.

## Mythological

All nuts represent wisdom, but the hazel in particular symbolizes knowledge. In Celtic myth, the hazel was credited with magical and divinatory powers and symbolized inspiration; Irish heralds displayed hazel rods as a symbol of office. Hazels were sacred to the Celtic sea god Manannan, which may be why mariners believed that hats of woven hazel twigs protected them in storms.

Such was the reverence with which the pagan Irish held the hazel that to destroy one was a capital offense. Gradually, however, as old ways and gods were abandoned, this sentence was commuted to the still hefty fine of a cow.

In Greek mythology, the rod carried by Hermes, messenger of the gods, was hazel wood, giving it the symbolism of communication and therefore reconciliation and peace, which spring therefrom. In Europe, hazel twigs were carried to claim protection because Hermes (Roman Mercury) was also god of roads and those who traveled on them* (see also **cherry, gourd** [in **melon**]).

In Scandinavian mythology, hazels were sacred to Thor, the Norse thunder god, and its connections with water gave it powers utilized in rain charms.

Hazels, **apples**, and **walnuts** were among grave-goods on the Oseberg, Norway, pagan ship-burial.

---

\* Appropriately, Hazel was the leader of the rabbits seeking a new home in Richard Adams' 1972 classic *Watership Down*.

# Symbolic Uses of the Hazel

- Recalling Greek symbolism of communication, appropriate for feast day of St. Bernardine of Siena, patron of communications personnel

- Recalling European connection with protection, appropriate for adoption; baptism; birth

- Recalling connection with souls, appropriate for All Saints Day; All Souls Day

- Recalling connection with water/rain, appropriate for harvest festival; Kwanzaa; planting; Rogation Days; Thanksgiving; and, recalling tradition that rain on his feast day foretells forty more wet days, also appropriate for St. Swithin's Day

- Recalling filberts, appropriate for St. Philibert's Day

- Recalling symbolism of knowledge, appropriate for beginning kindergarten/college/school; commencement; graduation

- Recalling symbolism of children, appropriate for children's birthdays; Children's Day; Holy Innocents Day

- Recalling popularity for kindling, appropriate for feast day of St. Elizabeth of Hungary, patron of bakers

- Recalling connection with Hermes, protector of travelers, appropriate for bon voyage; feast days of Sts. Christopher and Raphael, patrons of travelers; first driver's license; first step; homecoming (college); leaving home; pilgrimage; welcome home

- Recalling role in midsummer love-charm, appropriate for Midsummer's Day; Midsummer's Eve; St. Valentine's Day; summer solstice

# *Walnut*

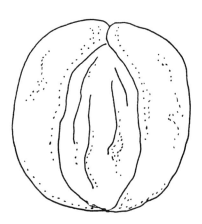

The walnut's botanical name, *Juglans regia*, translates loosely as "Jupiter's royal acorn," although the nut is probably a native of Turkey rather than Greece. Its common name is derived from the Old English "wealhhnutu," meaning "Welshman's nut," "Welsh" here meaning "foreign." By the Middle Ages, walnuts were indeed commonly known as "foreign nuts," and the term is still occasionally used in western England.

**Christian**    In Christian art, a divided walnut was emblematic of Mary and appears in this role in Joos van Cleve's highly symbolic *Virgin and Child with St. Joseph* (c. 1513; see also **cherry, pomegranate**; for other Marian symbolism, see **almond, apple, cherry, lemon, olive, raspberry, strawberry**).

A European folktale tells of St. Agatha sailing round the Mediterranean in a walnut shell, a story similar to a number of accounts of saintly voyages in unlikely objects, such as the millstone which brought St. Piran from Ireland to Cornwall. It may be only coincidence that her name is similar to that of St. Agathus (or Acacius), a Cappadocian martyr to whom Constantine the Great built a church in Constantinople. This church was nicknamed "The Walnut" because it was built round the walnut tree to which St. Agathus was tied for the whipping which preceded execution.

A curious eastern European legend relates that God had been eating walnuts during the Deluge, and that (although all but those aboard the Ark perished) many souls were saved by sailing to heaven in the empty walnut shells (see also **hazel**).

**Ethnic**    To the ancient Greeks and Romans, walnuts symbolized long life. They were also a nuptial celebratory food, and Pliny describes them as emblematic of marriage.

It was formerly the custom in the Poitou region of France to circle St. John's Eve bonfires while carrying walnut branches. A curious feature of the celebrations was the passing of walnuts to and fro over the flames; this was said to cure toothaches (see Medicinal; see also **apricot, fig, olive**).

In parts of Germany, fires of walnut, oak, and beech were kindled on Easter Saturday; charred sticks from these fires were taken home to protect dwellings from lightning.

Romanies (Gypsies) are said to use walnut dye to darken their skins.

The "butternut grey" of the Confederate Army's uniform during the American Civil War is usually derived from the suggestion that the dye used was from the shells of the nuts of the long or white walnut, *Juglans cinerea* (meaning, loosely, "Jupiter's ash-colored acorn"). The butternut's common name derived from its oily kernels.

European folklore claims that a heavy crop of walnuts foretells a harsh winter but also promises an excellent harvest the year after. Perhaps this has contributed to the nut's symbolic aspect of triumph over ill fortune or sorrow.

As with **almond, hazel,** and other nuts, walnuts also represent children.

## Literary/Artistic

A somewhat hostile traditional rhyme declares that, "A Woman, a Dog and a Walnut tree / The more you beat them, the better they be." In the case of the tree, it has been suggested that thrashing it destroys weakening offshoots which might otherwise have reduced its yield.

In his song about devising punishments to fit the crime, the title character in Gilbert and Sullivan's *The Mikado* (1885) declares that he has decreed that women who dye their hair will have their skin permanently dyed brown with walnut juice—a terrible fate in an era where pale skin represented not only beauty but also gentility.

Walnut wood has long been prized for furniture, veneers, and, in particular, gun stocks. The latter use inspired the colloquialism "shouldering walnut," meaning to enlist in the military.

**Medicinal**    In medieval medicine, preparations of walnut were prescribed for head injuries and mental illness. This followed the "Doctrine of Signatures," which stated that a plant resembling a bodily part would cure ailments thereof, for the walnut does bear a certain resemblance to the brain.

Recalling the French connection with teeth (see Ethnic), herbalists recommended walnuts for dogbites; Native Americans used medicine made from the black walnut, *Juglans nigra*, (loosely, "Jupiter's black acorn") for snakebites (see also **olive**).

A curious seventeenth-century cure for deafness was to place green walnuts in the ears, while carrying a spider in a walnut shell was considered effective against the ague and similar fevers. This charm is still practiced against rheumatism in parts of England today (see also **chestnut, raspberry**).

In North American herbal lore, walnut leaves were reckoned effective against household pests (see also **elderberry**), and English gardeners recommended their use against certain garden bugs.

**Mythological**    In Greek mythology, when the mortal Carya died, Dionysus, god of wine and merriment (who had loved her) turned her into a walnut tree (for a similar story about Phyllis, see **almond**). Carya gave her name to the caryatids, nymphs who were spirits of nut trees, and to the pillars in female form which support pediments in classical architecture (the best-known examples being those on the Erechtheum on the Acropolis in Athens).

Walnuts and **almonds** were eaten during festivals honoring Zeus' first wife, Metis.

Walnuts, **apples**, and **hazels** were among grave-goods found in the Oseberg, Norway, pagan ship-burial.

# Symbolic Uses of the Walnut

- Recalling symbolism of knowledge, appropriate for beginning kindergarten/college/school; commencement; graduation; reaching adulthood

- Recalling symbolism of children, appropriate for children's birthdays; Children's Day; Holy Innocents Day

- Recalling symbolism of triumph, appropriate for Election Day; men's festivals; peace celebration; promotion; reaching goal; taking office; women's festivals

- Recalling French custom, appropriate for first tooth; also appropriate for feast day of St. Apollonia, invoked against toothaches

- Recalling old name of "Welsh nut," appropriate for feast day of St. David, patron of Wales

- Recalling military connections, appropriate for Armed Forces Day; enlistment; military discharge; also appropriate for feast days of Sts. George and Martin, patrons of soldiers; Clement, patron of sailors; and Teresa of Lisieux, patron of aviators

- Recalling medicinal uses, appropriate for feast days of Sts. Dymphna, patron of the mentally afflicted, and Francis de Sales, patron of the deaf

- Recalling old name of "foreign nut," appropriate for new citizen; new immigrant; also appropriate for feast day of St. Frances Cabrini, patron of immigrants

- Recalling Marian symbolism, appropriate for Marian festivals

- Recalling legendary voyage, appropriate for bon voyage; launching; St. Agatha's Day; also appropriate for feast days of Sts. Christopher and Raphael, patrons of travelers

- Recalling German custom, appropriate for feast day of Sts. Barbara, invoked against lightning, and Erasmus (Elmo), invoked against storms

- Recalling gardening lore, appropriate for feast day of St. Fiacre, patron of gardeners

- Recalling Greek and Roman connection with longevity, appropriate for adoption; birth; family/general birthday; grandfather's birthday; grandmother's birthday; Grandparent's Day; long-service award; remarriage; retirement; wedding; wedding anniversary

- Recalling Deluge legend, appropriate for All Souls Day

# Appendix A:
## Fruits and Nuts for Weekdays, Based upon Mythology

| Day of Week | Latin Name | God/Goddess | Fruit/Nut |
|---|---|---|---|
| Monday | *dies Lunae* | Day of the Moon | Orange; pear[*] |
| Tuesday | *dies Martis* | Day of Mars, god of war | Cranberry; strawberry[**] |
| Wednesday | *dies Mercuri* | Day of Mercury, messenger of the gods | Hazel[***] |
| Thursday | *dies Jovis* | Day of Jove | Walnut[****] |
| Friday | *dies Veneris* | Day of Venus, goddess of love | Apple[+] |
| Saturday | *dies Saturni* | Day of Saturn | All fruits and nuts[++] |
| Sunday | *dies Solis* | Day of the Sun | Orange; tangerine[+++] |

[*]  Both fruits have lunar connections.

[**]  As red fruits, sacred to the god of war.

[***] Mercury was equated with Hermes, who carried a **hazel** rod.

[****] From botanical name of **walnut**, *Juglans regia*, loosely, "Jupiter's royal acorn," Jove being an alternative name for Jupiter.

[+]  **Apples** are sacred to love goddesses.

[++]  Saturn was an agricultural god.

[+++] Both fruits are sun symbols.

# Appendix B:
# Fruits and Nuts for Weekdays, Based upon Traditional Rhyme

| Day of Week | Attribute | Fruit/Nut |
| --- | --- | --- |
| Monday's child is fair of face | Beauty | Cherry; peach[*] |
| Tuesday's child is full of grace | Spiritual beauty | Olive; raspberry[**] |
| Wednesday's child is full of woe | Sorrow | Blackberry; elderberry[***] |
| Thursday's child has far to go | Travel | Coconut; banana[****] |
| Friday's child is loving and giving | Sweet-natured | Almond; strawberry[+] |
| Saturday's child works hard for a living | Industrious | Apple[++] |
| But the child that is born on the Sabbath Day is bonny and blithe and good and gay | Blessed | Peach; plum[+++] |

---

[*] Among fruits symbolizing beauty.

[**] Among fruits with Marian symbolism.

[***] Both considered fruits of ill omen.

[****] Both have connotations of faraway places.

[+] Symbols of sweetness of character.

[++] Representing humankind's fate to work after the Fall.

[+++] Among those trees considered to grow in Paradise.

# Appendix C:
## Fruits and Nuts for Months,
## Based upon Mythology, Custom, and Symbolism

| *Month* | *Fruit/Nut* | *Symbolism* |
| --- | --- | --- |
| January | Melon | New Year gift in Hong Kong and Singapore |
| February | Plum | Blossom represents February in Japanese floral calendar |
| March | Cherry | Represents spring; here symbol of spring equinox |
| | Peach; pear | Blossoms represent March in Japanese floral calendar |
| April | Pomegranate | Fruit symbolizes folly in Victorian flower language |
| May | Apple | Represents May Day, a workers' holiday, from the fruit's connection with humankind's fate to work after the Fall |
| June | Blackberry | Creek Indian name for June was Blackberry Month |
| | Strawberry | Traditional American name for June's full moon; here symbol of summer solstice |
| July | Apricot | Old rhyme connects July with apricots |
| August | Melon | Symbol of summer |
| September | Grape; olive | Carried by Greek figures of autumn; here symbols of autumn equinox |

| October | Chestnut | Creek Indian name for October was Big Chestnut Month |
| | Pumpkin | Traditionally connected with Halloween |
| November | Cranberry; pumpkin | Traditionally connected with Thanksgiving |
| December | Orange; tangerine | Sun symbols; here symbols of winter solstice |
| | Pomegranate | Greek symbol of death of year |

# Appendix D:
## Fruits and Nuts for Signs of the Zodiac,
## Based upon Mythology, Custom, and Symbolism

| *Sign* | *Symbol* | *Dates* | *Fruit/Nut* |
|--------|----------|---------|-------------|
| Aquarius | Water bearer | January 20 - February 18 | Watermelon (see melon) |
| Pisces | Fishes | February 19 - March 20 | Hazel[*] |
| Aries | Ram | March 21 - April 19 | Blackberry[**] |
| Taurus | Bull | April 20 - May 20 | Grape[***] |
| Gemini | Twins | May 21 - June 20 | Pear |
| Cancer (Moon Child) | Crab | June 21 - July 22 | Plum[****] |
| Leo | Lion | July 23 - August 22 | Orange[+] |

[*]  **Hazels** were sacred to Manannan, Celtic god of the sea.

[**]  Recalling the ram's traditional symbolism of stubbornness and the **blackberry's** role as emblematic of obstinancy.

[***] Recalling the **grape**vine, which sprang from the tail of the Bull killed by Mithras.

[****]Connected with the sea by the nickname "**plum** puddinger," used of a ship which took only short trips.

[+]  Like the lion, a traditional sun-symbol.

| | | | |
|---|---|---|---|
| Virgo | Virgin | August 23 - September 22 | Strawberry[*] |
| Libra | Scales | September 23 - October 22 | Chestnut[**] |
| Scorpio | Scorpion | October 23 - November 21 | Lemon[***] |
| Sagittarius | Archer | November 22 - December 21 | Gooseberry[****] |
| Capricorn | Goat | December 22 - January 19 | Olive[+] |

---

[*] One of many fruits with Marian symbolism.

[**] Connecting the scales of justice with the **chestnut's** Victorian symbolism of a plea for same.

[***] Here the proverbial sharpness of the **lemon** is transferred allegorically to that of the scorpion's sting.

[****] Recalling the use of goose-plumage for feathering arrows.

[+] Goats were anciently sacrificed to Greek Athene, goddess of wisdom, because they ate the leaves of her sacred **olive** tree.

# Appendix E:
## Fruits and Nuts for Saints' Feast Days

In general, the **date** is symbolic of the saints and martyrs. This chart points out specific saints or feast days, their dates, and their corresponding fruits/nuts.

| Saint/Feast | Date | Fruit/Nut |
|---|---|---|
| Agatha | February 5 | Walnut |
| All Saints Day | November 1 | Apple; chestnut; date; hazel |
| All Saints Eve | October 31 | Chestnut |
| Andrew | November 30 | Chestnut; lime (see lemon); watermelon (see melon) |
| Anne | July 26 | Cherry; raspberry |
| Apollonia | February 7 | Apricot; fig; olive; walnut |
| Barbara | December 4 | Cherry; walnut |
| Bernardine of Siena | May 20 | Hazel |
| Blaise | February 3 | Almond; black currant (see grape); persimmon; plum; raspberry |
| Camillus | July 18 | Apple; grapefruit; lemon; lime (see lemon); raspberry |
| Cecilia | November 22 | Elderberry; melon; peach; pear; quince |

| | | |
|---|---|---|
| Christopher | July 25 | Citron; date; hazel; melon; walnut |
| Clement | November 23 | Lemon; orange; plum; walnut |
| Constantine (Eastern Orthodox) | May 21 | Fig |
| David | March 1 | Lime (see lemon); walnut |
| Domitian | May 7 | Date; persimmon |
| Dorothy | February 6 | Apple |
| Dymphna | May 15 | Walnut |
| Elizabeth of Hungary | November 19 | Hazel |
| Erasmus (Elmo) | June 2 | Walnut |
| Eusebius of Vercelli | December 16 | Pear |
| Fiacre | September 1 | Fig; quince; walnut |
| Frances Cabrini | December 22 | Lime (see lemon); tomato; walnut |
| Francis | October 4 | Cranberry; elderberry; melon; raspberry |
| Francis de Sales | January 29 | Walnut |
| Gabriel | March 24 | Olive |

| | | |
|---|---|---|
| George | April 23 | Lime (see lemon); walnut |
| Giles | September 1 | Raspberry |
| Holy Innocents | December 28 | Almond; hazel; melon; strawberry; walnut |
| Honoratus of Arles | January 16 | Almond |
| Hubert | November 3 | Raspberry |
| James the Greater | July 25 | Chestnut; grape; melon; watermelon (see melon) |
| Joan of Arc | May 30 | Quince |
| John | December 27 | Chestnut; watermelon (see melon) |
| John the Baptist | June 24 | Strawberry |
| Joseph | March 19 | Apple; orange |
| Lucy | December 13 | Blackberry; pineapple; quince |
| Luke | October 18 | Apple; grapefruit; lemon; lime (see lemon); raspberry |
| Martin | November 11 | Chestnut; gooseberry; prune (see plum); walnut |
| Mary Magdalen | July 22 | Blackberry; elderberry; raspberry |
| Monica | May 4 | Apple |
| Nicholas | December 6 | Apple; lemon; orange |

| | | |
|---|---|---|
| Patrick | March 17 | Lime (see lemon); peach |
| Peter | June 29 | Chestnut; watermelon (see melon) |
| Philibert | August 20 | Hazel |
| Raphael | October 24 | Citron; gourd; hazel; melon; walnut |
| Raymond Nonnatus | August 31 | Cherry; raspberry |
| Saints Invoked Against Illnesses | | Apple; grapefruit; lemon; lime (see lemon); raspberry (See also Get Well Soon entry in Appendix F) |
| Simon | October 28 | Chestnut |
| Swithin | July 15 | Apricot; hazel; melon; plum |
| Teresa of Lisieux | October 3 | Walnut |
| Valentine | February 14 | Apple; apricot; grapefruit; hazel; orange; pomegranate; strawberry; tomato |
| Vitus | June 15 | Lemon |
| Yves | May 19 | Date; pear |
| Zita | April 27 | Apple |

# Appendix F:
## Index of Occasions

| **Occasion** | **Fruit/Nut** |
| --- | --- |
| Adoption | Apple; cherry; citron; coconut; fig; gooseberry; grape; hazel; melon; peach; pear; quince; raspberry; walnut |
| Advent | Gooseberry; grape |
| All Souls Day | Apple; cherry; date; hazel; pear; plum; quince; walnut |
| Anniversary of Loss | Apple; blackberry; elderberry; melon; pear; pomegranate (See also entry for Loss) |
| Anniversary of Wedding | *General:* Apple; citron; orange; pineapple; plum; quince; strawberry; walnut<br>*First:* Pear<br>*Fiftieth:* Orange |
| April Fool's Day | Elderberry; gooseberry; pomegranate |
| Arbor Day | All fruits and nuts, but in particular almond; fig; grape; olive; pomegranate |
| Armed Forces Day | Chestnut; gooseberry; lemon; orange; pineapple; prune (see plum); walnut |
| Ascension Day | Gooseberry; gourd (see melon) |
| Audit | Apple; blackberry; (white) cherry; elderberry; lemon; pear |

| | |
|---|---|
| Autumn Equinox | Chestnut; grape; olive; persimmon; pomegranate |
| Baby Shower | Apple; date; fig; gooseberry; orange; pomegranate; raspberry; strawberry |
| Baptism | Apple; date; grape; hazel; olive; orange; pomegranate; strawberry; watermelon (see melon) (See also entry for Namegiving) |
| Beginning kindergarten/ college/school | Almond; apple; cherry; fig; hazel; lemon; orange; walnut |
| Birth | Date (See also entry for Adoption) |
| Birthday | *Family/general:* Cherry; fig; grape; melon; orange; peach; pear; pineapple; raspberry; walnut *Boy:* Apple; banana; date; peach *Children:* Almond; elderberry; hazel; lemon; orange; pear; walnut *of Departed:* Almond; apple; blackberry; cherry; elderberry; melon; persimmon; pomegranate *Father:* Almond; cherry; pineapple *Father-in-law:* Almond; cherry; pineapple *Fifth:* Plum *Fortieth:* Blackberry; elderberry; lemon; raspberry *Girl:* Apricot; peach; pear; pomegranate *Grandfather:* Almond; cherry; pineapple; plum; walnut *Grandmother:* Apple; pineapple; plum; walnut *Mother:* Apple; pineapple *Mother-in-law:* Apple; blackberry; elderberry; lemon; pineapple *Over-the-Hill:* See entry for Fortieth. *Seventh:* Plum |

|  |  |
|---|---|
|  | *Sweet Sixteen:* Peach; plum; strawberry |
|  | *Teen:* Blackberry; pear |
|  | *Third:* Plum |
|  | *Twins:* Pear |
| Bon Voyage | Banana; coconut; hazel; lemon; lime (see lemon); olive; plum; quince; walnut |
| Bosses Day | Apple |
| Bridal Shower | Almond; apple; fig; gooseberry; orange; strawberry |
| Celebration of Life | Almond; apple; cherry; date |
| Children's Day | Almond; elderberry; hazel; lemon; melon; orange; walnut |
| Christmas | Almond; apple; cherry; cranberry; date; orange; pear |
| Columbus Day | Cranberry; lime (see lemon); pineapple; tomato |
| Commencement | Almond; apple; cherry; fig; hazel; lemon; olive; orange; walnut |
| Concert | Melon; peach; pear |
| Confirmation | Almond; apple; chestnut; grape; orange; pomegranate; strawberry |
| Congratulations | Orange; strawberry |
| Debut | *Artistic/professional:* Lemon; olive; orange |
|  | *Social:* Grape; lemon; olive; orange |
| Dedication | Elderberry; lemon; olive; watermelon (see melon) |

| | |
|---|---|
| Divorce | Blackberry; white cherry; elderberry; fig; gooseberry; grape; grapefruit; lemon; melon; raisin (see grape); raspberry |
| Earth Day | All fruits and nuts, but in particular chestnut; coconut; cranberry; date; fig; grape; pomegranate; pumpkin |
| Easter Sunday | Apple; date; orange; pear; quince |
| Election Day | Cherry; chestnut; date; pear; walnut |
| Engagement | Apple; fig; peach; plum; strawberry |
| Enlistment | Chestnut; gooseberry; lemon; orange; pineapple; prune (see plum); walnut |
| Epiphany | Almond; apple; cherry; date; orange |
| Farewell | Blackberry; elderberry |
| Father's Day | Almond; cherry; pineapple; raspberry |
| First... | *Driver's License:* Hazel; lemon; lime (see lemon); melon; olive<br>*Eucharist:* Almond; apple; chestnut; grape; orange; pomegranate; strawberry<br>*Fruits:* All fruits and nuts, but in particular grape; pumpkin; raspberry<br>*Haircut:* Gooseberry; pumpkin<br>*Step:* Hazel; lemon; lime (see lemon); melon; plum<br>*Tooth:* Apricot; fig; olive; walnut<br>*Word:* Lemon; plum; prune (see plum) |
| Flag Day | Cherry; cranberry |

| | |
|---|---|
| Friendship Day | Apple; grape; orange; pear; raspberry; strawberry |
| Fundraiser | Cherry; grape; olive; orange |
| Funeral | Apple; blackberry; cherry; coconut; date; elderberry; melon; peach; persimmon; plum; quince; raisin (see grape) |
| Get Well Soon | Apple; grapefruit; lemon; lime (see lemon); pear; plum; raspberry<br>(See also entry for Saints Invoked Against Illnesses, Appendix E) |
| Good Fortune | Apricot; cherry; coconut; melon; orange; persimmon; plum; strawberry |
| Good Friday | Blackberry; elderberry; grape; lemon; pomegranate |
| Graduation | Almond; apple; cherry; fig; hazel; lemon; olive; orange; walnut |
| Grandparent's Day | Almond; apple; cherry; pineapple; plum; raspberry; walnut |
| Groundbreaking | Cherry; lemon; orange; peach; pear; tangerine (see orange) |
| Groundhog Day | Cherry; orange; tangerine (see orange) |
| Halloween | Blackberry; elderberry; pumpkin |
| Harvest Festival | See entry for Thanksgiving. |
| Holocaust Memorial Day | Blackberry; elderberry |
| Homecoming (college) | Hazel; pineapple |
| Housewarming | Apricot; coconut; lemon; orange; peach; pear; pineapple; tangerine (see orange) |

| | |
|---|---|
| Independence Day | Cherry; cranberry; plum; pomegranate |
| Jury Duty | Chestnut; date; peach; pear |
| Kwanzaa | See entry for Thanksgiving |
| Labor Day | Apple |
| Launching | Banana; coconut; lemon; lime (see lemon); olive; orange; plum; walnut |
| Leaving Home | Coconut; hazel; lemon; lime (see lemon); olive; pear |
| Lent | Blackberry; chestnut; elderberry; pear |
| Lincoln's Birthday | Cherry; watermelon (see melon) |
| Long Service Award | Date; orange; walnut |
| Loss | Blackberry; elderberry; pear; raisin (see grape) (See also entry for Anniversary of Loss) |
| Lunar Eclipse | Apple; orange; pear |
| Marian Festivals | Almond; apple; cherry; lemon; olive; raspberry; strawberry; walnut |
| Martin Luther King, Jr., Day | Date |
| May Day | Apple; strawberry |
| Memorial Day | Almond; apple; cherry; grape; melon; pomegranate |

| | |
|---|---|
| Men's Festivals | Almond; banana; date; grape; plum; walnut |
| Midsummer's Day/Eve | Apple; blackberry; hazel; melon; orange; pear; strawberry; tangerine (see orange) |
| Milestones | Date; orange; strawberry |
| Military Discharge | Chestnut; gooseberry; lemon; orange; prune (see plum); walnut |
| Moon | *Full:* Apple; orange; pear; strawberry<br>*New/Quarter:* Apple; orange; pear |
| Mother-in-Law's Day | Apple; blackberry; elderberry; lemon |
| Mother's Day | Apple; pineapple; raspberry |
| Namegiving | Grape; olive; orange; watermelon (see melon)<br>See also entry for Baptism |
| Negotiation | Banana; cherry; olive; pear; plum |
| New... | *Citizen:* Apple; cherry; cranberry; lemon; lime (see lemon); orange; tangerine (see orange); walnut<br>*Home:* See entry for Housewarming<br>*Immigrant:* Lime (in lemon); orange; tangerine (see orange); tomato; walnut<br>*Job:* Apricot; cherry; lemon; olive; orange; pear; persimmon; plum; tangerine (see orange)<br>*Venture:* Apricot; cherry; coconut; lemon; olive; orange; peach; pear; persimmon; plum; tangerine (see orange) |

| | |
|---|---|
| New Year's Day/Eve | Apple; apricot; chestnut; lemon; melon; olive; orange; plum; pomegranate; tangerine (see orange) |
| Ordination | Almond; grape; olive; pomegranate; watermelon (see melon) |
| Palm Sunday | Apple; date; fig; orange |
| Peace Celebration | Banana; cherry; fig; grape; melon; olive; pear; pomegranate; raspberry; raisin (see grape); walnut |
| Pentecost | Pear; pomegranate |
| Pilgrimage | Almond; apple; chestnut; date; elderberry; hazel; melon; strawberry |
| Planting | All fruits and nuts, but in particular apricot; hazel; melon; orange; plum; tangerine (see orange) |
| Premiere | Date; lemon; lime (see lemon); olive; orange |
| Presidents' Day | Cherry; cranberry |
| Press Conference | Pumpkin |
| Promotion | Banana; date; melon; orange; plum; pumpkin; walnut |
| Reaching... | *Adulthood:* Almond; apple; cherry; date; orange; pineapple; walnut<br>*Goal:* Banana; coconut; date; melon; orange; peach; persimmon; plum; pumpkin; strawberry; walnut |
| Recital | See entry for Concert |
| Recognition Award | Date; orange; pumpkin; strawberry |

| | |
|---|---|
| Reconciliation | Banana; cherry; fig; melon; olive; orange; pear; pomegranate; raisin (see grape); strawberry; tangerine (see orange) |
| Recovery | See entry for Get Well Soon |
| Remarriage | Almond; apple; apricot; banana; chestnut; citron; fig; grape; lemon; olive; orange; peach; pear; pineapple; plum; quince; raspberry; strawberry; tangerine (see orange); walnut (See also entry for Wedding) |
| Remembering Departed | Almond; apple; blackberry; cherry; coconut; elderberry; melon; persimmon; pomegranate |
| Requiem | Almond; blackberry; cherry; coconut; elderberry; melon; persimmon; pomegranate; raisin (see grape) |
| Retirement | Orange; peach; plum; strawberry; walnut |
| Retreat, religious | Date; fig; tomato |
| Reunion | *College/High School:* Chestnut; orange<br>*Family:* Almond; chestnut; pineapple |
| Rogation Days | Cherry; chestnut; hazel; melon; orange; plum; tangerine (see orange) |
| School Play | Lime (see lemon) |
| Secretaries' Day | Apple; elderberry |
| Separation | Blackberry; white cherry; elderberry; fig; gooseberry; grape; grapefruit; lemon; melon; pineapple; raspberry; raisin (see grape) |

| | |
|---|---|
| Shrove Tuesday | Chestnut; strawberry |
| Solar Eclipse | Orange; tangerine (see orange); peach |
| Sports Victories | Date; elderberry; gooseberry; horse chestnut (see chestnut); orange; pear; plum; strawberry |
| Spring Equinox | Almond; cherry; chestnut; peach; pomegranate |
| Statehood Day | Plum; pomegranate |
| Summer Solstice | Apple; apricot; blackberry; hazel; melon; orange; peach; pear; plum; pomegranate; strawberry; tangerine (see orange) |
| Sweetest Day | Almond; pear; raspberry; strawberry |
| Taking Office | Chestnut; date; elderberry; pear; walnut |
| Thanksgiving | All fruits and nuts, but in particular citron; coconut; cranberry; date; fig; grape; hazel; olive; orange; plum; pomegranate; pumpkin; tangerine (see orange) |
| Trinity Sunday | Date; strawberry |
| Veterans' Day | Cherry |
| Wake | Apple; cherry; coconut; date; elderberry; melon; peach; persimmon; plum; pomegranate; raisin (see grape) |
| Washington's Birthday | Almond; cherry |

| | |
|---|---|
| Wedding | Almond; apple; apricot; banana; chestnut; citron; fig; grape; lemon; orange; peach; pear; pineapple; plum; quince; raspberry; strawberry; walnut<br>(See also entry for Remarriage) |
| Welcome... | *Home:* Citron; hazel; melon; pineapple<br>*New Baby:* Cherry; date; fig; pineapple |
| Winter Solstice | Citron; fig; orange; persimmon; plum; pomegranate; pumpkin; tangerine (see orange) |
| Women's Festivals | Apple; apricot; fig; grape; peach; plum; pomegranate; strawberry; walnut |

# Bibliography:
## Fruitful Sources for Further Study

Although I have occasionally gone out on a limb (doubtless of **plum** wood,
representing independence) in translating and/or interpreting information,
those titles marked with an asterisk are nonetheless fruitful sources for further
study by those who are interested in the basic premise of this book.

**Botany**    Bailey, Liberty H. *Hortus Third.* New York: Macmillan Publishing Co., 1976.

*Banana Times.* Washington, D.C.: International Banana Association, 1989.

*Book of the British Countryside.* London: Drive Publications, 1973.

*California Strawberry Advisory Board Press Kit.* Watsonville, California, 1990.

Coon, Nelson. *Using Plants for Healing: An American Herbal.* Emmaus, Pennsylvania: Rodale Press, 1979.

Everett, Thomas H., ed. *The New York Botanical Gardens Illustrated Encyclopedia of Horticulture.* New York: Garland Publishing, Inc., 1980.

*Extraordinary Cherry, The.* Okemos, Michigan: Cherry Marketing Institute, n.d.

Hamel, Paul, and Mary Chiltoskey. *Cherokee Plants: Their Uses and History.* Ashville, North Carolina: Hickory Printing Co., n.d.

Kadans, Joseph M. *Encyclopedia of Medicinal Herbs, with the Herb-o-Matic Locator Index.* New York: Arco Publishing Co., 1972.

Limburg, Peter. *What's In the Names of Fruit.* New York: Coward, McCann & Geoghegan, 1972.

Palmer, E. Laurence, and H. Seymour Fowler. *The Field Book of Natural History.* New York: McGraw-Hill Book Co., 1975.

*Romance of Pears, The.* San Francisco: Pacific Coast Canned Pear Service, n.d.

*Romancing the Date.* Indio, California: California Date Admnistrative Committee, 1987.

Schuler, Stanley. *Simon & Schuster's Guide to Trees.* New York: Simon & Schuster, 1978.

*Strawberry Great Ideas.* Watsonville, California: California Strawberry Advisory Board, 1990.

Ethnic Allard, William Albert. "Chinatown: The Gilded Ghetto." *National Geographic* (November 1975).

*Austria Folk Customs.* Vienna, Austria: Federal Press Service, 1985.

Bauer, Helen, and Sherman Carlquist. *Japanese Festivals.* Garden City, New York: Doubleday & Co., 1965.

Bendann, Effie. *Death Customs: An Analytical Study of Burial Rites.* Ann Arbor, Michigan: Gryphon Books, 1971.

Brauns, Claus-Dieter. "Peaceful Mrus of Bangladesh." *National Geographic* (February 1973).

Brown, Ivor, ed. *A Book of England.* Glasgow, Scotland: Collins, 1971.

Clibbon, Joan. *Cooking the British Way.* London: Paul Hamlyn, 1963.

de Garis, Frederic. *We Japanese.* Miyanoshita, Japan: Fujiya Hotel, 1946.

Gillison, Gillian. "Fertility Rites & Sorcery in a New Guinea Village." *National Geographic* (July 1977).

Goodale, Jane C., and Anne Chowning. "Blowgun Hunters of the South Pacific." *National Geographic* (June 1966).

Itasaka, Gen, ed. *The Kodansha Encyclopedia of Japan*. Tokyo: Kodansha Ltd., 1983.

Kunstadter, Peter. "Living with Thailand's Gentle Lua." *National Geographic* (July 1966).

Liman, Ingmar. *Traditional Festivities in Sweden*. Stockholm: Swedish Institute, n.d.

Sanchez, M. A. *Celebrating in Spain*. Madrid: Secretaria General de Turismo, 1986.

Singh, Anne de Henning. "Sea Gypsies of the Philippines." *National Geographic* (May 1976).

*Small Treasury of Swedish Food, A*. Stockholm: Swedish Dairies Association, 1985.

Taki, Shodo. *Japan Today*. Tokyo: Society for Cultural Information, 1948.

Wentzel, Volkmar. "Zulu King Weds a Swazi Princess." *National Geographic* (January 1978).

## Folklore

Blacker, Carmen. "The Stranger: Consideration of a Disguised Wandering Saint." *Folklore 1990* II. London: The Folklore Society, 1990.

Chaundler, Christine. *Every Man's Book of Superstitions*. New York: Philosophical Library, 1970.

Coffin, Margaret. *Death in Early America: The History and Folklore of Customs and Superstitions of Early Medicine, Funerals, Burials and Mourning*. Nashville, Tennessee: Nelson, 1976.

de Lys, Claudia. *A Treasury of American Superstitions*. New York: Philosophical Library, 1948.

"Notes & Queries." *F.L.S. News* (January 1991). London: The Folklore Society.

Philipose, Lily. "The Twa Sisters: A Santal Folktale Variant of the Ballad." *Folklore 1990* II. London: The Folklore Society, 1990.

## History

Brønstadt, Johannes. *The Vikings.* Harmondsworth, United Kingdom: Penguin Books, 1960.

Buxton, David. *The Abyssinians.* London: Thames & Hudson, 1970.

Chadwick, Nora. *The Celts.* Harmondsworth, United Kingdom: Penguin Books, 1970.

Coleman, William L. *Today's Handbook of Bible Times and Customs.* Minneapolis, Minnesota: Bethany House Publishers, 1984.

Davidson, Marshall B., ed. *The Horizon Book of Lost Worlds.* New York: American Heritage Publishing Co., 1962.

Freed, Rita. *Ramses the Great: The Pharaoh and His Times.* City of Memphis, Tennessee: 1987.

Graves, Robert, and Alan Hodge. *The Long Weekend: A Social History of Great Britain.* Harmondsworth, UK: Penguin Books, 1971.

Gurney, O. R. *The Hittites.* Harmondsworth, United Kingdom: Pelican Books, 1952.

Holmes, Reg, and Mike Rouse. *Ely: Cathedral City and Market Town. A Pictorial Record 1817-1934.* Ely, United Kingdom: The Ely Society, 1972.

*Last Two Million Years, The.* Pleasantville, New York: Reader's Digest Association, 1979.

## Language, Literature, and The Arts

Aldington, Richard, ed. *The Viking Book of Poetry of the English-Speaking World.* New York: Viking Press, 1941.

Auboyer, Jeannine. *Oriental Art: A Handbook of Styles and Forms.* Translated by Elizabeth & Richard Bartlett. New York: Rizzoli, 1980.

Baring-Gould, William S. and Ceil. *The Annotated Mother Goose.* New York: Bramhall House, 1962.

Betteridge, Harold T. *The New Cassell's German Dictionary.* London: Cassell & Co. Ltd., 1962; New York: Funk & Wagnalls, 1958.

Drabble, Margaret, ed. *Oxford Companion to English Literature.* Oxford: Oxford University Press, 1985.

Evans, Ivor H., ed. *Brewer's Dictionary of Phrase and Fable.* New York: Harper & Row, 1981.

Gilbert, A., and W. S. Sullivan. *The Plays of Gilbert and Sullivan.* Garden City, New York: The Book League of America, Garden City Publishing Company Inc., 1941.

Gillison, Gillian and David. "Living Theater in New Guinea's Highlands." *National Geographic* (August 1983).

Girard, Denis. *The New Cassell's French Dictionary.* London: Cassell & Co. Ltd.; New York: Funk & Wagnalls, 1962.

Graves, Robert. *The White Goddess: A Historical Grammar of Poetic Myth.* London: Faber & Faber, Ltd., 1971.

Hibbard, Howard. *The Metropolitan Museum of Art.* New York: Harrison House, 1980.

Hindley, Geoffrey, ed. *Larousse Encyclopaedia of Music.* London: Hamlyn Publishing, 1986.

Horcasitas, Fernando. "Mexican Folk Art." *National Geographic* (May 1978).

Jacobs, Sidney J. *The Jewish Word Book.* Middle Village, New York: Jonathan David, 1982.

Lacy, Norris J., ed. *The Arthurian Encyclopedia.* New York: Peter Bedrick Books, 1986.

Lewis, Charlton T., and Charles Short. *Harper's Latin Dictionary.* Rev. ed. New York: American Book Company, 1907.

Martin, Michael R., and Richard C. Harrier. *Concise Encyclopedic Guide to Shakespeare.* New York: Horizon Press, 1971.

Mencken, H. L. *The American Language: An Enquiry into the Development of English in the United States*. New York: Alfred A. Knopf, 1971.

Morley, Christopher. *The Standard Book of British and American Verse*. Garden City, New York: Garden City Publishing Co. Inc., n.d.

*Oxford Dictionary of Quotations*. Oxford: Oxford University Press, 1986.

Rosten, Leo. *The Joys of Yiddish*. Harmondsworth, United Kingdom: Penguin Books, 1971.

Sears, Minnie Earl, ed. *Song Index to More Than 12,000 Songs in 177 Song Collections Comprising 262 Volumes*. New York: H. W. Wilson Company, 1926.

Simpson, D. P. *Collin's New Compact Latin Dictionary*. New York: Laurel Books, 1974.

Spevack, Marvin. *Harvard Concordance to Shakespeare*. Cambridge, Massachusetts: Harvard University Press, 1973.

Stableton, Michael. *The Cambridge Guide to English Literature*. Cambridge, United Kingdom: Cambridge University Press, 1983.

Tatlock, John S. P., and Arthur G. Kennedy. *A Concordance to the Complete Works of Geoffrey Chaucer and the Romaunt of the Rose*. Gloucester, Massachusetts: Peter Smith, 1963.

Wernecke, Herbert H. *Christmas Songs & Their Stories*. Philadelphia: Westminster Press, 1957.

## Mythology

*Aldington, Richard, and Delano Ames, trans. *New Larousse Encyclopedia of Mythology*. New York: Putnam, 1968.

Avery, Catherine B. *New Century Handbook of Greek Mythology and Legend*. New York: Appleton-Century-Crofts, 1972.

*Cavendish, Richard, ed. *Man, Myth, and Magic*. New York: Marshall Cavendish, 1983.

Ellis Davidson, H. R. *Gods & Myths of Northern Europe*. Harmondsworth, United Kingdom: Penguin Books, 1964.

*Facts on File Encyclopedia of World Mythology and Legend*. New York: Facts on File, 1988.

Grant, Michael, and John Hazel. *Gods and Mortals in Classical Mythology*. Springfield, Massachusetts: G & C Merriam, 1973.

Graves, Robert. *Greek Myths*. London: Cassell & Co., 1969.

Gray, John. *Near Eastern Mythology*. London: Hamlyn Publishing Group, 1975.

*Leach, Maria, ed. *Funk & Wagnalls Standard Dictionary of Folklore, Mythology, and Legend*. New York: Funk and Wagnalls, 1972.

O'Flaherty, Wendy, trans. *Hindu Myths*. Harmondsworth, United Kingdom: Penguin Books, 1975.

Oswalt, Sabine G. *Concise Encyclopaedia of Greek and Roman Mythology*. Glasgow, Scotland: Collins, 1969.

Robinson, Roland. *Aboriginal Myths & Legends: Age-Old Stories of the Australian Tribes*. London: Paul Hamlyn, 1969.

*Walker, Barbara G. *The Woman's Encyclopedia of Myths & Secrets*. New York: Harper & Row, 1983.

## Religion

Allen, Clifton J., ed. *The Broadman Bible Commentary*. Nashville, Tennessee: Broadman Press, 1972.

Asimov, Isaac. *Asimov's Guide to the Bible: The Old Testament*. New York: Avon Books, 1968.

_____. *Asimov's Guide to the Bible: The New Testament*. New York: Avon Books, 1969.

Attwater, Donald. *The Penguin Dictionary of Saints.* Harmondsworth, United Kingdom: Penguin Books, 1965.

Broderick, Robert C. *The Catholic Encyclopedia.* Nashville, Tennessee: Thomas Nelson, 1976.

Brown, Raymond C., ed. *New Jerome Biblical Commentary.* Englewood Cliffs, New Jersey: Prentice-Hall, 1990.

Bryant, T. Alton, ed. *New Compact Bible Dictionary.* New York: Pillar Books, 1976.

Cohen, Abraham. *Everyman's Talmud.* New York: Schocken Books, 1978.

Crim, Keith, ed. *Interpreter's Dictionary of the Bible.* Nashville, Tennessee: Abingdon, 1976.

Delaney, John. *The Dictionary of Saints.* Garden City, New York: Doubleday, 1980.

Eliade, Mircea, ed. *The Encyclopedia of Religion.* New York: Macmillan, 1987.

Foy, Felician A., ed. *Catholic Almanac.* Huntington, Indiana: Our Sunday Visitor Publishing, 1990, 1991.

Frazer, Sir James G. *The Golden Bough: A Study in Magic and Religion.* London: Macmillan, 1970.

Gaskell, G. A. *Dictionary of All Scriptures and Myths.* New York: Avenel Books, 1981.

Humphreys, Christmas. *Buddhism.* Harmondsworth, United Kingdom: Penguin Books: 1990.

Kanof, Abram. *Jewish Ceremonial Art and Religious Observance.* New York: Harry N. Abrams Inc., 1970.

Lippman, Thomas W. *Understanding Islam: An Introduction to the Muslim World.* New York: Mentor Books, 1990.

Miller, Madeleine S., and J. Lane. *The New Harper's Bible Dictionary.* New York: Harper & Row, 1973.

Newman, Louis J., and Samuel Spitz. *The Talmudic Anthology: Tales and Teachings of the Rabbis: A Collection of Parables, Folk tales, Fables, Aphorism, Epigrams, Sayings, Anecdotes, Proverbs and Exegetical Interpretations.* New York: Behrman House, 1966.

Pickthall, Mohammed Marmaduke. *The Meaning of the Glorious Koran: An Explanatory Translation.* New York: Mentor Books, n.d.

Rice, Edward. *Eastern Definitions.* Garden City, New York: Doubleday & Co., 1978.

Roth, Cecil, ed. *Encyclopedia Judaica.* Jerusalem: E. J. Keter Publishing House Ltd.; New York: Macmillan Co., 1972.

Stroup, Herbert. *Like a Great River: An Introduction to Hinduism.* New York: Harper & Row, 1972.

Teas, Jane. "Temple Monkeys of Nepal." *National Geographic* (April 1980).

Thurston, Herbert, and Donald Attwater. *Butler's Lives of the Saints.* Westminster, Maryland: Christian Classics, Inc., 1981.

## Symbolism

*Cooper, J. C. *Illustrated Encyclopaedia of Traditional Symbolism in Western Art.* London: Thames & Hudson, 1978.

Drake, Maurice. *Saints and Their Emblems.* Chicago: Gale Publishing, 1971.

Eberley, Susan. "The Hawthorn in Medieval Love Allegory." *Folklore 1989* I. London: The Folklore Society, 1989.

*Hangen, Eva. C. *Symbols, Our Universal Language.* Wichita, Kansas: McCormick-Armstrong, 1962.

**Kate Greenaway's Language of Flowers.* New York: Gramercy Publishing, 1978.

*Powell, Claire. *The Meaning of Flowers: A Garland of Plant Lore and Symbolism from Popular Custom and Literature.* Boulder, Colorado: Shambhala Publishers, Inc., 1979.

*Walker, Barbara G. *The Woman's Dictionary of Symbols and Sacred Objects.* New York: Harper & Row, 1988.

Whittick, Arnold. *Symbols, Signs and Their Meaning.* Newton, Massachusetts: Charles T. Branford, 1960.

Whittlesey, E. S. *Symbols and Legends in Western Art: A Museum Guide.* New York: Charles Scribner's Sons, 1972.

*Williamson, John. *The Oak King, The Holly King, and The Unicorn: The Myths and Symbolism of the Unicorn Tapestries.* New York: Harper & Row, 1986.

Travel

"Discoverers of the Pacific." A map supplement in *National Geographic* (December 1974).

Gordon, Robert. "Papua New Guinea: Nation in the Making." *National Geographic* (August 1982).

Graves, William. "Bangkok, The City of Angels." *National Geographic* (July 1973).

Grosvenor, Melville Bell. "The Isles of Greece." *National Geographic* (August 1972).

de la Haba, Louis. "Belize, The Awakening Land." *National Geographic* (January 1972).

*Illinois' Historic Lincoln-Logan County.* Lincoln, Illinois: Tourism Bureau of Logan County, 1990.

Keating, Bern. "Pakistan." *National Geographic* (January 1967).

La Fay, Howard. "Portugal at the Crossroads." *National Geographic* (October 1965).

MacDowell, Bart. "The Aztecs." *National Geographic* (December 1980).

MacLeish, Kenneth. "Java—Eden in Transition." *National Geographic* (January 1971).

Michael, Sabina & Roland. "Trek to Lofty Hunza—and Beyond." *National Geographic* (November 1975).

Mitchell, Carleton. "French Riviera: Storied Playground on the Azure Coast." *National Geographic* (June 1967).

Muller, Kal. "Taboos & Magic Rule Namba Lives." *National Geographic* (January 1972).

Patterson, Carolyne Bennett. "100 Years Later: Travels with a Donkey." *National Geographic* (October 1978).

de Roos, Robert. "The Philippines, Freedom's Pacific Frontier." *National Geographic* (September 1966).

Weaver, Kenneth F. "Maui, Where Old Hawaii Still Lives." *National Geographic* (April 1971).

General Reference    *Chamber's World Gazeteer*. Edinburgh, Scotland: Chambers, 1988.

Cosman, Madeleine Pellner. *Fabulous Feasts: Medieval Cookery and Ceremony*. New York: George Brazillier Inc., 1976.

Coyle, L. Patrick. *World Encyclopedia of Food*. New York: Facts on File, 1982.

*Funk & Wagnalls New Encyclopedia of Science*. Milwaukee, Wisconsin: Raintree Publications, 1986.

Montaigne, Prosper. *Larousse Gestronomique: The New American Edition of The World's Greatest Culinary Encyclopedia*. New York: Crown Publishers, 1988.

*New American Desk Encyclopedia*. New York: Signet Books, 1989.

*New American Webster Handy College Dictionary*. New York: Signet Books, 1981.

*New Encyclopaedia Britannica, The*. Chicago: Encyclopaedia Britannica Inc., 1987.

*Oxford English Dictionary,* compact ed. Oxford: Oxford University Press, 1971.

Panatti, Charles. *The Browser's Book of Beginnings: The Origins of Everything Under (and Including) the Sun.* Boston: Houghton-Mifflin Co., 1984.

Parise, Frank, ed. *The Book of Calendars.* New York: Facts on File, 1982.

*Random House Dictionary of the English Language.* New York: Random House, 1987.

Seltzer, Leon E., ed. *Columbia Lippincott Gazeteer of the World.* Morningside Heights, New York: Columbia University Press, 1952.

*Strange Stories, Amazing Facts.* Pleasantville, New York: Reader's Digest Association, 1978.

Urdang, Laurence. *Holidays and Anniversaries of the World.* Detroit: Gale Research Co., 1975.

*Webster's New Collegiate Dictionary.* Springfield, Massachusetts: G. & C. Merriam, 1975.

*World Book Encyclopedia.* Chicago: World Book Inc., 1990.

*World's Last Mysteries, The.* Pleasantville, New York: Reader's Digest Association, 1978.